MW01517805

Diverse Pedagogical Approaches to Experiential Learning, Volume II

Karen Lovett
Editor

Diverse Pedagogical Approaches to Experiential Learning, Volume II

Multidisciplinary Case Studies, Reflections, and Strategies

Editor
Karen Lovett
Office of Experiential Learning
University of Dayton
Dayton, OH, USA

ISBN 978-3-030-83687-0   ISBN 978-3-030-83688-7   (eBook)
https://doi.org/10.1007/978-3-030-83688-7

This Palgrave Macmillan imprint is published by the registered company Springer Nature Switzerland AG.
The registered company address is: Gewerbestrasse 11, 6330 Cham, Switzerland

For Ophelia

FOREWORD: BEYOND THE ANSWER OF EXPERIENTIAL LEARNING—RAISING QUESTIONS FOR TRANSFORMATIVE TEACHING AND LEARNING

Experiential learning (EL) has certainly captured the attention and imagination of many educators in the last several decades. Whether through the lens of community-based learning, study abroad, community immersions, project-based learning, or work-integrated learning experiences, educators across sectors have looked to EL as a potential strategy to engage students in education. In effect, EL has been the answer to many education-related questions. *How do you engage students in deep, meaningful learning?* In the context of higher education, EL has been the response from the lens of student engagement with high-impact learning (Kuh, 2008), as well as the lens of pedagogy with course frameworks for significant learning (Fink, 2013). *What are the career outcomes of a college graduate and value of a college degree?* EL has also been the answer to career-related outcomes questions and a response to the value of a college education and degree (Hora et al., 2016). In summary, EL sometimes serves as a response to a variety of questions emerging from higher education.

Yet, EL, in practice, is complicated and messy. It requires planning and intentionality around teaching and learning practices. The coordination of outside partners and/or places and spaces may be involved, as well as *multiple* forms of reflection on the experiences. The National Society for Experiential Education (NSEE) has provided eight principles of good practice (www.nsee.org/8-principles) which include intentionality, preparedness and planning, authenticity, and reflection, just to name a select few. The clearly defined principles demonstrate the complexity of implementing strong experiential learning programs and courses. The one principle, however, that always strikes me when I review them, is authenticity, defined as:

> The experience must have a real world context and/or be useful and meaningful in reference to an applied setting or situation. This means that it should be designed in concert with those who will be affected by or use it, or in response to a real situation. (www.nsee.org/8-principles)

This reference to the "real world context" or "an applied setting or situation" relates as much to the teaching context as it does to the learning context. Here lies the potency of this second volume of *Diverse Pedagogical Approaches to Experiential Learning: Multidisciplinary Case Studies, Reflections, and Strategies,* as it situates the chapters as answers to many teaching and learning questions, while authentically raising questions about EL practice.

This edited volume is indeed a collection of case studies, from a specific context of the University of Dayton (UD), authored by EL practitioners and educators from a variety of disciplines, including social work, education, law, biology, humanities, and business. The EL practitioners draw from various educational support areas, including campus ministry, and leadership offices in the context of UD. Amid the reflections upon the complexity of implementing EL, the authors in this volume extract the vulnerability and authenticity it takes to be teachers and learners in experiential education.

The collection of interdisciplinary, transdisciplinary, and multidisciplinary approaches of experiential education makes this volume unique, as it stems from a singular institutional context. It explores the degree to which EL serves to align an institution's academic programs, curriculum, and programming with its mission. Since UD is a faith-based institution, this context also inherently interrogates the degree to which faith intersects with community engagement and other forms of EL, as personal and professional experiences inform and influence faith-based contexts of learning (Green et al., 2020).

In addition, the emphasis on collaborative projects and EL practitioners also contributes to distinguishing this edited volume on experiential education. At its essence, EL is collaborative as the learner is often learning in relation to an experience, one's peers, the community setting, community members, organizational partners, and the educator. The collaborative projects and cross-disciplinary approaches described in various chapters define inherent characteristics of EL as multidisciplinary. As the voices of EL practitioners are elevated as educators and implementers of experiential education, the volume captures its authenticity by connecting examples to real-life scenarios found in higher education.

As we turn to that idea of authenticity, this volume recognizes that good EL with real-world issues is messy—and that is the intersection where good learning and good teaching reside. The chapters explore the transformative teaching and learning of experiential education, not as an approach that is neatly pre-packaged with a bow, but rather as a complex, challenging, and process-oriented pedagogy that is always evolving. The authors in the edited volume, *Diverse Pedagogical Approaches to Experiential Learning: Multidisciplinary Case Studies, Reflections, and Strategies,* do not share easy answers, but rather raise many more questions about the pedagogy of EL in order to keep reflecting and improving their practice. With this in mind, perhaps EL is the answer to another question—*how do you build transformative learning and transformative teaching?*

Loyola University Chicago
Chicago, IL, USA   Patrick M. Green

REFERENCES

Green, P. M., Stewart, C. P., Bergen, D. J. & Nayve, C. (2020). Faith and community engagement at anchor institutions: Exploring the intersection and turning toward an engagement of hope. *Metropolitan Universities, 31*(3), 3–21.

Fink, L. D. (2013). *Creating significant learning experiences: An integrated approach to designing college courses.* Jossey-Bass.

Hora, M. T., Benbow, R. J., & Oleson, A. K. (2016). *Beyond the skills gap: Preparing college students for life and work.* Harvard Education Press.

Kuh, G. D. (2008). *High-impact educational practices: What they are, who has access to them, and why they matter.* Association of American Colleges and Universities.

National Society for Experiential Education. (2019). *Eight principles of good practice for all experiential learning activities* (para. 1–8). https://www.nsee.org/8-principles. Accessed 22 Mar 2021.

ACKNOWLEDGMENTS

I would like to thank my family, friends, and colleagues for their support to this project. Thanks to my husband Justin and beautiful daughter Ophelia for bringing me joy every day and cheering me on. Thanks to my mom, Ligia, and sister Sandra for teaching me to love writing and learning. I am especially grateful to all the authors who contributed to this collection, and our talented group of assistant editors: Anna Biesecker-Mast, Maggie Cahill, Beth Hock, Christina Mesa, Abigail Neal, and Emily Schmitz. I am thankful for their hard work, ingenuity, and collaborative spirit. I am also grateful to Associate Provost Deb Bickford for her mentorship and advice. Our conversations have inspired me to bring these stories and reflections about EL together so we can (in Deb's words) "make teaching and learning community property." I appreciate the support and leadership of UD President Eric Spina and Provost Paul Benson. I also thank all my wonderful colleagues in the Ryan C. Harris Learning Teaching Center, and all the campus and community partners whose innovative EL initiatives have truly benefited so many students' lives. Thank you to the editors at Palgrave for helping this project become successful.

CONTENTS

Notes on Contributors

Adrienne Ausdenmoore (BFA, MBA) is the founding director of the Institute of Applied Creativity for Transformation (IACT) at the University of Dayton, an academic institute training students in creative problem-solving, critical thinking, and cross-disciplinary collaboration. In her role, Ausdenmoore fosters learning strategies in applied creativity and transdisciplinary learning inclusive of students, faculty, and staff across disciplines. She has over 15 years of experience in education innovation, where she has developed and managed innovative learning spaces, led strategic visioning initiatives, and designed experiential learning and vocational discernment opportunities. She teaches The Practice of Applied Creativity and Design Your Life courses, and is part of the global community of University educators teaching life design that originated at Stanford University's d.school.

Anna Biesecker-Mast is a junior honors student at the University of Dayton, working toward a BA in English and History along with minors in Religious Studies and Women's and Gender Studies. During the summer of 2020, she worked as a Communications Associate and Field Intern for a local Congressional campaign while also researching for her Dean's Summer Fellowship project. This year, she began her honors thesis in the History department—which focuses on the history of Black women and mothers in the United States. Specifically, she is searching creative nonfiction accounts for their historical resistance in systems of constraint and oppression.

Maggie Cahill is a senior English major with a self-designed Composition and Literature concentration and a minor in Marketing at UD. She was a member of the ENG 377 EL course that participated in the editing process of the book's first volume and returns to this volume as Editorial Assistant. As a member of the University Honors Program, her thesis involves a self-study in editorial decision-making in which she edits a fellow student's sports memoir. She has served as a reviewer for UD's *Line by Line*, a student journal in which her work has also been published. Additionally, she has served as a copywriter for *Spectrum News 1 (KY)* broadcasts. She is a member of the Sigma Tau Delta International English Society and a varsity athlete on UD's rowing team. She plans to pursue a Masters of Education at the University of Notre Dame through the ACE Teaching Fellows program.

Nick Cardilino is Associate Director of Campus Ministry and Director of the Center for Social Concern. Cardilino has been Campus Minister at the University of Dayton since 1991. As Director of the Center for Social Concern, he and his colleagues provide students, faculty, and staff with a wide variety of opportunities to do community service and social justice work and reflect on those experiences in light of their faith. He also teaches a course on Faith and Justice in the Religious Studies Dept. He received his MA in Theology from UD in 1989.

Mario D'Agostino is a PhD and is Assistant Professor of Writing in the Department of Communication, Media, and the Arts at Nova Southeastern University. His work focuses primarily on archives, curation, and museology, arguing that curation is a necessary part of our lives and knowledge formation. His work on writing in the archives has been recently featured in the Writing Spaces online archives. D'Agostino is the Managing Editor for *Experiential Learning & Teaching in Higher Education (ELTHE)*.

Irene J. Dickey is Principal Lecturer in Marketing in the School of Business Administration at the University of Dayton. She has taught a variety of business classes for 30 years and has been utilizing a broad scope of experiential learning strategies in the classroom and out. She believes that the process of education through experience, followed by reflection on that experience, truly enhances the overall learning experience. She has been publishing marketing content but has recently expanded into experiential learning.

Kevin Dvorak holds a PhD and is the Executive Director of the NSU Writing and Communication Center, Faculty Coordinator for First-Year Experience, and Professor in the Department of Communication, Media, and the Arts at Nova Southeastern University. He is a past president of both the International Writing Centers Association and the Southeastern Writing Center Association. Dvorak is the Editor-in-Chief of *Experiential Learning & Teaching in Higher Education* (*ELTHE*) and Senior Editor for the *Journal of Faculty Development*.

David J. Fine is Assistant Professor of English at the University of Dayton. His research focuses on sex, secularization, and ethics in the modern British novel, and he teaches courses in twentieth-century fiction, LGBTQ+ literature, and feminist theory. He has published on issues surrounding religion, queerness, and critical pedagogy.

Catherine Lawless Frank holds an EdD and is Assistant Professor of Teacher Education at the University of Dayton in the School of Education and Health Science. She teaches in the Intervention Specialist program and has spent over 25 years in education. Her scholarship and interests focus on teacher preparation, experiential learning, special education, and inclusion.

Patrick M. Green holds an EdD and serves as the Executive Director (and Founding Director) of the Center for Experiential Learning (CEL) at Loyola University Chicago, overseeing the service-learning, academic internships, undergraduate research, and learning portfolio programs. Green also serves as a clinical assistant professor in the School of Education at Loyola University Chicago. Green teaches a variety of general elective experiential learning courses, engaging students in service-learning, community-based research, international service-learning, internship experiences, and undergraduate research. He completed a co-edited volume focused on the intersections of faculty development and service-learning/community engagement entitled *Re-conceptualizing faculty development in service-learning/community engagement: Exploring intersections, frameworks, and models of practice* (2018), Green serves as an Engaged Scholar with National Campus Compact and he serves as the Scholar-in-Residence with IARSLCE and as an Engaged Scholar with the National Society for Experiential Education (NSEE).

Beth Hock is a senior attending the University of Dayton, graduating in the Spring of 2021 with a BA in English. With a Self-Designed concentration, she focuses her studies on Teaching, Design/Fine Arts, Creative Writing, and Editing/Publishing. Hock helped organize and edit the first volume of this publication, and returns as Editorial Assistant working in the Office of Experiential Learning. She is on the review board for *Line By Line*, a journal of student writing and also works with the Marian Library on campus.

Jesse Hughes is the 5th year PhD student in Biology. Hughes is National Science Foundation Graduate Research Fellow whose research is focused on understanding how genes are regulated over the course of animal development. As an undergraduate at the University of Dayton (UD) he participated in the first cohort of the Creating Inclusive Community initiative. He along with three of his peers formed the University's Creating Inclusive Community Conference to engage the community in conversations of equity and inclusion on UD's campus. Hughes was involved in the CIC program for six years before moving on to his current role as the Associate Director of the McNair Scholars program at Knox College.

Shelley Inglis is the Executive Director of the Human Rights Center and Research Professor of Human Rights and Law. She is a practitioner with an over 20-year career in international affairs having served in the United Nations Development Programme, the Office of the United Nations Deputy Secretary-General, the Department of Peacekeeping Operations, the Office of the High Commissioner for Human Rights in Geneva, the United Nations Development Fund for Women (UNIFEM), Organization for Security and Cooperation in Europe (OSCE) (1999–2002) in Kosovo, Amnesty International Secretaria, and Save the Children US. Her expertise is in policy guidance and program support related to peacebuilding, rule of law, democratic governance, human rights and gender equality, and women's empowerment. She has also practiced public interest family and criminal law in the United States and served as an adjunct professor at Barnard College. She is a graduate of Columbia School of Law (JD) as a Kent Scholar, and Cornell University (BA).

Samantha Kennedy holds an MA and MPA. She is the Coordinator of Community Engagement in the University of Dayton's Center for Social Concern. In addition to her MA degree in Theological Studies, and Master of Public Administration degree, she has her Certificate in Nonprofit and Community Leadership. In her work, she strives to connect students with individuals and organizations in the Dayton community. She hopes students can learn with their community and become leaders who help build the common good and put their faith into action for social justice. Her areas of focus include Active Citizenship, Catholic Social Teaching, and Leadership for the Common Good.

Brian LaDuca is a 2017 Dayton Forty Under 40 award winner and the founding Executive Director of the Institute of Applied Creativity for Transformation (IACT) at the University of Dayton. His research is focused on the creative skills gaps in today's emerging workforce. As faculty Executive Director, he leads the developing applied creative microcredentials and badges for all University of Dayton students, faculty, and staff, and steers the ongoing city-wide collaboration of The GEM, Dayton's experimental learning space innovating education as a creative and experiential tool in combating inequities within the city. Since 2015, he has presented his research and work across the world including keynote presentations and workshops in Mexico, Switzerland, Peru, and China.

Karen Lovett is the Director of Experiential Learning in the Office of Experiential Learning at the University of Dayton. She works with faculty, staff, students, and community partners to support the development of EL opportunities across the university. In her role, she also oversees an EL innovation grant, supports EL research and scholarship initiatives, and develops methods of EL reflection and assessment. She works with students to expand awareness of EL opportunities and generate dialogue about the ways EL connects to their personal, academic, and vocational goals. Karen is interested in how people learn through experience in diverse social contexts, and her work highlights the transformative impact of experiential learning on students' and educators' lives. She has also taught courses on co-operative education, cultural anthropology, research methods, and organizational theory. She has a PhD in Anthropology and Education from Teachers College, Columbia University in the City of New York.

Mary McLoughlin has graduated from the University of Dayton in 2020 with a BA in Human Rights Studies and English Literature and minors in Women and Gender Studies and Political Science. She is a PhD student at Syracuse University studying political science with particular interest in the ways gender and sexuality shape the national and international and structure practices of citizenship and belonging.

Christina Mesa is a senior at the University of Dayton, preparing to graduate with a Bachelor's in English and concentration in Professional & Technical Writing. During her Junior year she worked as a student editorial assistant on Diverse Pedagogical Approaches to Experiential Learning volume one. This experience led to her pursuit and success in attaining a part-time role as an editorial assistant in the Office of Experiential Learning at the University of Dayton during her senior year. Through hard work and perseverance these academic successes have transferred to professional development and the mastery of written and verbal communication in the workplace.

Tom Morgan is the Director of Race and Ethnic Studies and Associate Professor of English at the University of Dayton. His research focuses on critical race theory in late nineteenth-century American and African American literature, specifically as it applies to the politics of narrative form, as well as African American haiku and the work of Paul Laurence Dunbar. In the classroom, he pushes students to connect the theory they read to the practice of their daily lives in order to develop skills that will help make them agents of change. He is also moderately obsessed with metaphor.

Abigail Neal is Senior English Major with a concentration in Rhetoric and Composition as well as a Philosophy Minor at the University of Dayton. Besides serving as an Editorial assistant, Neal has also worked as a Marketing and Social Media intern as well as a Managing Editing intern for an online publishing company. Next year she hopes to obtain a job in publishing in the hopes of one day being able to publish her own fictional writing.

Mary Niebler has served as the Coordinator of Cross-Cultural Immersions at the University of Dayton since 2006. Through her work, she hopes to provide diverse options for outreach, learning, and cultural exchange for students at UD on trips domestically and abroad. Mary enjoys working with motivated students, faculty, and staff who are willing to do something different with their break times and contribute toward a sense of global solidarity. She has a BS in Education and an MA in Theological Studies, both from the University of Dayton.

Carrie Rogan-Floom is a scholar-practitioner, having served students in diverse K-16 settings as a language arts teacher, an education consultant, a faculty mentor, and as a teacher educator and university liaison at the University of Dayton. She earned a BA and MEd from The Ohio State University and a PhD in Educational Leadership from the University of Dayton. Her focus is working with diverse populations to identify opportunities for growth and to provide support that will empower them to achieve their personal, academic, and professional goals.

Molly Malany Sayre is Assistant Professor of Social Work at the University of Dayton, where she teaches social work courses on communities, health, and advocacy. She often utilizes community-engaged learning in her courses, and she is an instructor of Inside-Out Prison Exchange Program classes. In addition to the scholarship of community-engaged learning, her research and practice focus is on maternal and child health equity and reducing infant and maternal mortality. She is especially interested in reducing maternal stress due to racism and economic inequality as a means of improving maternal and infant vitality and quality of life.

Denise Platfoot Lacey holds a JD and MSE. She is Professor of Externships at the University of Dayton School of Law. The courses she teaches include Externships, Professional Responsibility, and Law as a Calling. In her teaching, she emphasizes reflective practice as a skill and value of the legal profession. She hopes to instill in students an appreciation for reflection as a tool for enriching their lives as legal professionals. Her research interests include the formation of professional identity, vocation, EL pedagogy, and technology-enhanced learning. Prior to teaching, she practiced law where she investigated allegations of professional misconduct by lawyers and promoted professionalism among Ohio's attorneys and judges.

Emily Schmitz is a Senior English major with a concentration in Professional and Technical Writing at the University of Dayton (UD). In addition to her role as an Editorial Assistant for the Office of Experiential Learning at UD, she has also been a reviewer on the editorial board for UD's *Line by Line: A Journal of Beginning Student Writing* for a year and a half. She has a passion for using the writing skills she has developed as an English major to help others improve their written works. After graduation, she hopes to pursue a career in editing.

Yvonne Sun holds a PhD and is an associate professor in the Department of Biology at the University of Dayton. Sun is a microbiologist whose research area focuses on host-pathogen interactions and how environmental factors such as oxygen and fermentation acids influence these interactions. She teaches a variety of microbiology courses, including lecture courses such as general microbiology, biology of infectious disease, and applied microbiology and seminar courses such as biology of *Listeria* and biology of short-chain fatty acids. She is also the faculty coordinator for the general microbiology laboratory course.

Castel Sweet is a sociologist who explores the intricacies of community, culture, and race. Through her work as a community engagement professional, she encourages the unknown to be explored, endeavors to make the unfamiliar familiar, and seeks to cultivate relationships that are transformational instead of transactional. Castel's formal training in sociology enables her to comprehensively develop, support, and advocate for ethical and appropriate community-campus collaborations and community engagement at the collegiate level.

Joy Willenbrink-Conte holds an MA and MT-BC. She is Lecturer of Music Therapy at the University of Dayton, supervises pre-clinical training, and teaches music therapy degree courses, including Introduction to Music Therapy, Functional Music Therapy Skills, Professional Development for Music Therapists, Improvisation and Receptive Methods of Music Therapy, and Music and Psychotherapy. Her clinical experience is centered in mental health care of all ages, specifically addiction, trauma, and grief recovery. Central to her identity as a teacher, she continues her own practice as a music therapist in the Dayton, OH region. Her scholarship explores the nature of women's therapy groups, music therapy as addictions treatment, and considerations in music therapy training and education. Along with Susan C. Gardstrom, she co-authored *Music Therapy with Women with Addictions* (2020), Barcelona Publishers. She strives to be a lifelong learner and is immensely grateful for opportunities to learn from and alongside her students.

LIST OF TABLES

CHAPTER 1

Introduction: Ongoing Deliberations on the Meaning and Value of EL

*Karen Lovett, Anna Biesecker-Mast, Maggie Cahill,
Beth Hock, Christina Mesa, Abigail Neal,
and Emily Schmitz*

The field of experiential learning (EL) is changing along with our current times. Despite our increasingly digitized global interconnectedness, individuals entering college today are more acutely aware than ever of the ways communities around the world are divided. In response, many students feel called to be agents of change, to engineer solutions for the biggest challenges facing humanity. Experiential educators have an incredibly important role to play in creating opportunities for students to apply their knowledge in meaningful ways and discover relevance, purpose, and passion in their educational pursuits. As students and educators strive to achieve greater impact through EL, the boundaries of EL continue to

K. Lovett (✉) • A. Biesecker-Mast • M. Cahill • B. Hock • C. Mesa • A. Neal
• E. Schmitz
Office of Experiential Learning, University of Dayton, Dayton, OH, USA
e-mail: klovett1@udayton.edu; bieseckermasta1@udayton.edu

© The Author(s), under exclusive license to Springer Nature
Switzerland AG 2022
K. Lovett (ed.), *Diverse Pedagogical Approaches to Experiential
Learning, Volume II*,
https://doi.org/10.1007/978-3-030-83688-7_1

expand with new and innovative pedagogical approaches. In the process, it is important to reflect on the areas of opportunity as well as the challenges we face in the field of EL. Whether it be developing awareness and understanding of increasingly diverse student demographics, ensuring greater equity and inclusion in experiential programs, striving toward more sustainable, ethical EL models and reciprocal community partnerships, or advancing institutional support for experiential educators at all levels—whether they be tenured professors, staff members, adjuncts, or lecturers—these are just a few examples of the important and complex issues that form part of the context of our work.

Teaching and learning experientially are dynamic and continuously evolving processes, and the work of EL is never finished. As the narratives contained in the collection demonstrate, EL can often be messy and unsettling, while also illuminating and inspiring, for both students and educators. This book is a unique assemblage of EL reflections, case studies, and strategies written by faculty, staff, and graduate student educators at the University of Dayton (UD) in Dayton, Ohio. These EL examples range from community-engaged learning and project-based learning, to practicums, externships, education abroad, simulations, and more. Building upon the first volume (Lovett, 2021), these chapters describe how educators develop, implement, facilitate, expand, and assess EL in a variety of university courses, programs, and centers. The collection also introduces new perspectives on the intersections of EL with race, privilege, cross-cultural competencies, gender and feminism, vocation, spirituality, social justice, human rights, and more.

The volume includes a total of 28 authors, including 9 faculty, 8 staff, and 8 students across 16 academic departments and units of the University of Dayton (UD), including English, Women and Gender Studies, Campus Ministry, Law, and more. The book also features three authors and collaborators from Loyola University Chicago and Nova Southeastern University in Florida, who contributed their unique and important EL insights in the book foreword and afterword. The multidisciplinary nature of this collection underscores the importance of collaboration across disciplinary boundaries, and the benefits of learning from, and alongside, colleagues who come from diverse backgrounds, experiences, and areas of expertise. The benefits of bringing together such a varied group of experiential educators to exchange insights and strategies are many; this collective endeavor has helped us work toward enhancing student learning and supporting student success, while building a dynamic community that aims to contribute to positive social change and the common good through EL.

The volume also reflects UD's commitment to student-centered learning. A team of six students worked as assistant editors and played an integral role in developing and refining the book, as an EL project of its own. In the process, they gained experience doing editorial work and expanded their knowledge of EL, while also serving as peer mentors to each other. Indeed, student involvement in the two volumes has been critical—their voices and perspectives contribute truly valuable insights and awareness of areas for improvement and continued exploration.

The range of EL examples presented in the collection demonstrate that our authors do not define EL by a specific type of activity or program—internships or co-ops—for example, but rather by a shared set of principles that give EL meaning and structure, as well as a certain open-endedness that comes with learning through experience. As the chapters illustrate, EL is a process that involves active engagement and self-guided learning in a purposeful, immersive experience, as well as reflection and sense-making about that experience, in order to transform it into knowledge that can be applied in subsequent experiences and contexts. The educators in this collection encourage their students to be explorers, to take the lead, to have agency in their learning. They also realize that doing EL often entails giving up a certain amount of control to their students in the process. They also serve as mentors and advisors, guiding students through EL and helping them make meaning of their experiences. They encourage students to become reflective learners and listeners, and they challenge students to deeply consider how they can use and apply the knowledge they've gained through EL. In the process, experiential educators become more reflective practitioners themselves. Each of the chapters presented in this collection demonstrates an artful, intentional, and creative approach to teaching and learning, and each of them has helped students grow and transform in the process.

THE OFFICE OF EXPERIENTIAL LEARNING AND THE UNIVERSITY OF DAYTON

From engineering and chemistry labs to teacher education programs in Dayton schools and robust employment and internship opportunities in local businesses, hands-on learning has been an integral part of UD for many years. As a continuation of this long-standing commitment to EL, the Office of Experiential Learning (OEL) at UD opened in 2016, and has supported faculty and staff in the development of numerous EL initiatives and programs. In my role as Director of Experiential Learning, I have also created spaces for authors in this collection to share their work with the broader campus community through a series of virtual reading sessions and conversations over the course of the academic year. During these ongoing sessions, authors present on topics featured in their chapters and engage in dynamic dialogue with virtual guests. Offering multiple opportunities for individuals to come together and learn from one another has been an effective way to build and deepen EL community, highlight and acknowledge EL accomplishments, as well as advance the mission and vision of the university. These sessions also serve as educational forums that inspire colleagues to collaborate on new initiatives, develop their own programs, and explore areas of EL outside their own disciplines and areas of expertise.

The OEL also works with students through workshops called "EL Labs," intended to encourage students to develop holistic and integrative narratives about their various EL experiences and how they connect to personal, academic, and professional goals, using creative mapping and digital storytelling tools. In some ways, this book has been a form of "EL Lab" for authors, who engaged in their own storytelling through the process of writing about their EL teaching experiences, their vocations, their sense of purpose and passion behind their work, and the different pathways that brought them to where they are today.

The OEL also supports students at all stages of their college journey as they navigate the many EL opportunities available to them and explore post-graduation pathways that build on the EL experiences they've had. At UD, students have access to a variety of EL activities and programs that are integrated in the university curriculum (e.g., through our Common Academic Program) and co-curriculum, across numerous departments, centers, and institutes on campus. These EL experiences are guided by UD's institutional learning goals (ILGs), particularly Practical Wisdom and Vocation, which aim to prepare students with skills to apply their knowledge and discern their sense of calling and discover their passion and purpose. Many UD students are deeply engaged in EL off campus, around the city of Dayton and across the US, as well as internationally, through a variety of employment, internship, co-op, community-engaged learning, and education abroad opportunities. The incredibly collaborative environment at UD among educators, both faculty and staff, has led to the development of innovative interdisciplinary and transdisciplinary forms of EL. The OEL supports initiatives that arise from collaboration through access to grants, consultation on project design, support in the development of reflection and assessment techniques, publishing opportunities for EL scholarship of teaching and learning, and other resources.

As a Catholic, Marianist institution, UD is dedicated to the education of students for the common good, with a focus on the holistic development of learners—through connecting head, hand, and heart. Students are often attracted to UD because of its focus on community and the tangible ways they can make a difference and influence positive social change through EL. UD is constantly innovating and creating more unique opportunities for learning beyond the classroom. For example, through initiatives like the recently opened Hub in the downtown Dayton Arcade, which offers a dedicated space for community-engaged learning and entrepreneurship initiatives, students now have more opportunities than ever to connect with diverse people and industries, and gain real-world experience addressing some of the most pressing challenges facing local and global communities.

COMMUNITY ENGAGEMENT AND BUILDING RELATIONSHIPS BEYOND THE CLASSROOM

Section I, "Community Engagement and Building Relationships Beyond the Classroom," demonstrates the value of working with various community partners such as non-profits, NGOs, community centers, and others, and developing opportunities for students to learn from the experience and expertise of community leaders locally and globally. The chapters in this section also demonstrate effective ways of guiding students through the complex contexts they encounter through community-engaged learning. Chapter 2, *Community-Engaged Learning: Sticky Learning About the Social World* by Molly Malany Sayre, describes how community-engaged learning experiences with various partners including a church, a neighborhood development organization, and a correctional institution deepen learning by creating opportunities for authentic interactions. Through these interactions, students become emotionally invested in the learning process and expand their understanding of the complexities of the social world. Chapter 3, *Desperate Times Call for Experiential Learning: The*

Evolution of the Community Agency Project by Catherine Lawless-Frank, describes the creation of the Collaborative Agency Projects (CAP), an EL project that partners small groups of students with area agencies to develop and implement collaborative projects. As a result of this initiative, students develop trusting relationships, greater self-awareness, and more effective communication skills.

Chapter 4, *Human Rights Education Through Experiential Learning* by Shelley Inglis, provides an overview of the Human Rights Center's numerous domestic and international EL programs, including a partnership with a New York-based non-governmental organization (NGO) through which students explore human rights issues in Ferguson, Detroit, and Appalachia. This chapter also describes a research practicum with an NGO in Malawi focused on sustainable development as well as an anti-trafficking coalition focused on awareness, training, and prevention efforts with partners in the Miami Valley, Ohio. Like the other chapters in this section, Inglis' chapter highlights the importance of collaboration and building partnerships beyond the classroom to effectively empower students to affect social action and change.

FOSTERING ENTREPRENEURSHIP, CREATIVITY, AND PROBLEM-SOLVING SKILLS

Section II, "Fostering Entrepreneurship, Creativity, and Problem-Solving Skills," focuses on EL programs that encourage students to develop creative problem-solving and professional development skills through exposure to innovative research, project-based learning, and simulation-based activities, as well as through interactions with real-world clients and alumni in diverse sectors of the business world. Chapter 5, *Alumni Engagement Through Applied Creativity: A Case Study* by Brian LaDuca and Adrienne Ausdenmoore, discusses how they connect students to alumni through the Institute for Applied Creativity for Transformation (IACT) certificate program. In the process of engaging with alumni and completing their transdisciplinary cornerstone projects, IACT students gain real-world insights and experiences that connect to their own vocations.

Chapter 6, *An Experiential Learning Revolution: Engaging Business Students with Diverse Digital and Non-Digital Immersive Experiences with Not-for-Profit and for-Profit Organizations* by Irene Dickey, illustrates how EL is beneficial for students with different learning styles. Through client projects and digital simulations, Irene's marketing courses embed EL activities that heighten students' engagement and curiosity. Chapter 7, *Experiential Learning in Laboratory Courses: Reflections on the Tiny Earth Curriculum* by Yvonne Sun, describes the integration of the Tiny Earth curriculum, a global network of antibiotic discovery researchers, into her biology courses. Yvonne's chapter demonstrates how innovative and creative EL activities that are meaningful and relevant to students have a powerful impact on students' sense of resilience, ownership, purpose, as well as confidence in their decision-making abilities.

RACE, GENDER, FAITH, AND CROSS-CULTURAL PERSPECTIVES IN EXPERIENTIAL LEARNING

The chapters in Section III, "Race, Gender, Faith, and Cross-Cultural Perspectives in Experiential Learning," highlight how EL educators prompt students to partake in self-inquiry and critical reflection on diverse religious, racial, ethnic, gender, and cultural identities and perspectives and the ways in which identities often intersect and change over time. EL experiences can also bring to light the difficult and challenging realities of discrimination, systemic injustice, and social inequality, and the authors in this section discuss how they effectively navigate these subjects with students. Chapter 8, *Leveraging Experiential Learning to Create Inclusive Community at Predominantly White Institutions* by Castel Sweet, Tom Morgan, and Jesse Hughes, discusses the development of a course on privilege, diversity, and inclusion, in which students attend a White Privilege Conference. Through this EL experience, students engage in diversity and inclusion efforts and work to create and implement change on a predominantly white campus. Chapter 9, *393 Guineas: A Dialogue on Experiential Learning and Feminist Theory* by David Fine and Mary McLoughlin, provides a behind-the-scenes view of a project-based approach to learning about feminist theory and methodology. The authors offer insights on how staff and faculty with backgrounds in the humanities can integrate the practical skills of grant writing and advocacy with a theoretical analysis of social injustice. Chapter 10, *Learning from Faith-based Cross-cultural Immersions* by Nick Cardilino, Samantha Kennedy, Mary Niebler, demonstrates the ways EL immersions and community-engaged learning opportunities can help students deepen their spirituality and faith life. Their chapter, like others in this section, also offers valuable insights on how to guide students as they encounter economic inequality, social and political injustice, and environmental realities they most likely have never seen or experienced before.

SUPPORTING STUDENT DEVELOPMENT THROUGH MENTORSHIP AND REFLECTION

The chapters in Section IV, "Supporting Student Development Through Mentorship and Reflection," outline strategies for developing and enhancing two fundamental aspects of effective EL: mentorship and reflection. Providing robust support and guidance, as well as ample opportunities for reflective inquiry, can have a powerful impact on students as they engage in new EL experiences. Through mentorship and reflection, experiential educators are able to model trusting and reciprocal relationships and encourage students to find their authentic voices. Chapter 11, *Nurturing Learning Through the Pre-clinical Music Therapy Supervision Relationship* by Joy Willenbrink-Conte, identifies several key aspects involved in supporting students' development through pre-clinical training in a music therapy program. Her approaches help students explore their identities, while also deepening intrapersonal and interpersonal learning for both student and supervisor.

Chapter 12, *Assigning Reflection in Experiential Learning for Professional Formation* by Denise Platfoot Lacey, describes best practices for facilitating meaningful reflective practice for students engaged in law externships. Lacey demonstrates the importance of explaining the purpose of reflective practice to students and providing a framework for the reflective process in order to help them explore their professional identities. Chapter 13, *Encouraging Growth Through Experiential Education: Contributions of a Teacher Educator* by Carrie Rogan-Floom, highlights support strategies for guiding students through experiential fieldwork experiences in a teacher education program. Her chapter attends to the personal, academic, and professional challenges students experience as they enter and become part of new communities through their fieldwork.

LESSONS AND TAKEAWAYS

The sections of the book outlined above are not mutually exclusive, and there is an overlap in the topics and themes presented throughout the chapters. Important aspects of EL such as building relationships and community, creating meaningful and purposeful opportunities for dialogue and reflection, linking EL to relevant social issues and challenges, as well as finding effective ways to guide and mentor students in their development as leaders, for example, can be found throughout different chapters and sections in the book. Rather than offering answers about the "right" way to do EL, the chapters in this collection explore how educators experiment and refine their pedagogical approaches to EL, and how they experience challenges and transformations alongside their students. EL involves an ongoing process of "learning to learn," and frequent deliberations about the goals and meanings we ascribe to EL:

> people do discuss how to learn, and how to teach. Instructing, explaining, imagining are fundamental activities. Human life cannot proceed without instructions, and instruction about instructions. The fundamental issue concerns the work of learning about learning—what I gloss as 'education'. (Varenne, 2019)

Many experiential educators often begin with a particular goal or purpose in mind, but end up adapting their approach as a result of challenges or impromptu situations that emerge. What works for one group of students may not work for another group—educators may face resistance, unintended outcomes, or outside challenges that make it necessary to go back to the drawing board and figure out what comes next. The narratives presented in this book illustrate that "the human situation is educative, and that every new moment is necessarily the next occasion for learning" (McDermott & Raley, 2007).

Additionally, it is important to consider students' holistic learning by taking a larger view of their college activities and experiences. Students are often involved in a myriad of curricular and experiential activities, and learning happens across distinct environments and contexts both on and off campus. Learning should not be seen as a singular or individual process, but rather a communal and collective process that involves "continuity of experience," which according to John Dewey, one of the foundational philosophers of EL theory and practice, "means that every experience both takes up something from those which have gone before and modifies in some way the quality of those which come after" (Dewey, 1938, p. 13). Just as students make their way through varied experiences each day, this book takes readers on a path through an interconnected EL landscape at UD. We are connected as experiential educators and learners who share a common passion and interest in creating innovative and impactful EL.

In OEL workshops, we often draw connections between our past, present, and future experiences, and the lessons we learned along the way. We shape integrative narratives and examine the relevance of various learning moments in our lives, then visually map out these experiences on paper and digitally. Often, after seeing examples of students' "learning journey roadmaps," colleagues express interest in replicating this visual mapping for their own lives and experiences. Taking a moment to acknowledge the experiences that have held educational value for us in our lives and reflecting on how those experiences have shaped (and continue to shape) us is always a valuable endeavor because EL is a lifelong process. Guided by our own experiences, we are all in search of the greater purpose in our work in and through education.

References

Dewey, J. (1938). *Experience and education*. Macmillan.

Lovett, K. (2021). *Diverse pedagogical approaches to experiential learning: Multidisciplinary case studies, reflections, and strategies*. Palgrave Macmillan.

Mcdermott, R., & Raley, J. D. (2007). Discussion: From John Dewey to an anthropology of education. *Teachers College Record, 109*, 1820–1835.

Varenne, H. (2019). *Educating in life: Educational theory and the emergence of new normals. Routledge research in education*. Routledge.

Community Engagement: Building Relationships Beyond the Classroom

CHAPTER 2

Community-Engaged Learning: Sticky Learning About the Social World

Molly Malany Sayre

Experiential learning (EL) found me as a young adult. As a high school senior, I attended a retreat that incorporated group initiatives, a series of group challenges designed to foster communication and team building. The premise was often ridiculous, such as the group needing to cross a field of imaginary lava with only two pairs of imaginary lava-impervious shoes to share, and additional challenges were often added, like when the tallest group member was no longer allowed to use their arms when the challenge was for the group to get all members over a ten-foot wall. While sometimes uneasy with how physical the exercises were as compared to my perceived lack of physical strength, I was fascinated by what happened when the group "debriefed" the initiative at its end. The facilitators led discussions about participants' feelings during the activity, including at the points where it seemed like the group would fail; communication patterns, such as whose ideas were considered and whose were dismissed; and how

M. M. Sayre (✉)
Sociology, Anthropology, and Social Work, University of Dayton, Dayton, OH, USA
e-mail: msayre2@udayton.edu

© The Author(s), under exclusive license to Springer Nature Switzerland AG 2022
K. Lovett (ed.), *Diverse Pedagogical Approaches to Experiential Learning, Volume II*,
https://doi.org/10.1007/978-3-030-83688-7_2

individuals supported each other during the activity. The depth of the insights that these conversations produced fascinated me (I had no idea we had been ignoring her the whole time! How interesting that some of us respond to frustration with greater effort while others withdraw!). Facilitating group initiatives in ways that fostered this kind of learning about group dynamics, awareness of others, and feelings of closeness with my group seemed like a superpower at the time, but I knew it was a skill, and I knew it was one I desperately wanted to learn.

So after high school, I got a summer job as a camp counselor. Like most academics, I've had minimal formal instruction in teaching, but my summers working with children at a camp are the foundation for how I approach education, the art of teaching, and group leadership. As a camp counselor, I learned group facilitation skills, albeit mostly through on-the-job, all-eyes-are-on-me, trial-and-error experiences—a stretch for someone who had never taken a test she hadn't studied for. The lack of formal training forced me to hone the very skills I needed for effective group facilitation: watching and listening. To be ready to "work the magic" of the debrief, I observed the group's actions that followed patterns and the actions that didn't, paid attention to individuals' and teams' changes in and diversity of emotions, and listened for what was said and what wasn't. These observations allowed the debriefing questions to center on the group's experiences, drawing out participants' thoughts and feelings, insights, and questions, about the experience they had just shared. I watched teams grow more inclusive, individuals grow more confident, and leaders become more aware when facilitating—in other words, I saw groups learn. This is how EL found me.

This fascination with group dynamics, combined with a desire to work for social justice and tackle social issues, propelled me into the social work profession and specifically, social work education, when in graduate school. Put simply, I love the classroom. I enjoy few professional activities more than facilitating an engaging discussion of some aspect of the social world and watching astute students push each other to understand the causes of our current reality and ethical responses to it. And as a professor, when it comes to educating passionate adults, most of them adolescents, about the social world, I return to my teaching roots, cultivated at summer camp: I rely on experiential education, specifically community-engaged learning (CEL).

CEL is at the confluence of critical pedagogy, active learning, and Freire's (1993) dialogic model of education (Nagda et al., 2003). CEL promotes civic engagement, anti-oppressive action, democratic participation, and education through repeated cycles of action and reflection. It is often conducted in partnership with a community organization in a relationship of mutual benefit and reciprocity. Social work education, in most instances, prepares students to enact professional values, which include social justice and service (National Association of Social Workers, 2017), by promoting the well-being of vulnerable individuals, families, groups, and communities. Thus, there is a natural alignment between CEL and social work education. In short, one of the most authentic ways to educate social work students is through CEL.

In my academic career, I have attempted a variety of CEL partnerships. Some have been more successful than others. Some have lasted for multiple semesters, and others have ended after only one. Common themes among the more successful experiences have been achieving "sticky learning" through recognition of emotions in EL, which I discuss first; next, achieving learning that I can't effectively teach students on my own; and finally, the importance of reflection. In my teaching practice as a social work educator, these are the elements that keep my work engaged in the present, fresh for myself and my students, and relevant to the needs of the world and the interests of (most) students.

Sticky Learning

Back at summer camp, before we started a teambuilding activity, we would encourage participants to consider their comfort, challenge, and panic zones. Ryan (2006) describes these zones as comfort, stretch, and stress. One's comfort zone is an emotional "place" of security and ease, while one's panic zone is the experience of being overwhelmed by fear. Neither of these zones are conducive to learning. In our comfort zones, we are often not aware or focused enough to gain new insights or have an experience upon which we can reflect. In our panic zones, we are hyperfocused on getting out of the situation, causing panic to the point that we cannot observe or reflect upon anything else. (For example, the fear I felt when I fell out of the boat when whitewater rafting long ago taught me only that I never want to go whitewater rafting again.)

In between the comfort and panic zones, however, is one's challenge zone. In this emotional space, we are a little outside our normal environment or behavior, which allows us to be more aware of what we're experiencing and what's going on around us. This focus, then, permits us to reflect more deeply later and learn more from what we experienced. We remember these experiences, and what we learned from them, longer, too. What we learn when in our challenge zones sticks with us.

Studies of the neuroscience of learning and memory provide evidence for this theory. Emotions are essential to learning because they direct our mental energy to things that are important (Immordino-Yang, 2016). This has been evolutionarily adaptive for our species (Immordino-Yang, 2016; Polk, 2018): our emotions have kept us procreating, for instance, and steered us away from actual or potential sources of trauma, as experienced in the panic zone. In experiences with very little emotion, it is difficult for us to focus our attention for prolonged periods and achieve deep learning (death by PowerPoint comes to mind). However, short-term emotional arousal, as experienced in the challenge zone, has been shown to improve memory consolidation and focus our attention on relevant aspects of the experience (Polk, 2018). One reason EL is effective, then, is that it is likely to engage students' emotions and result in learning that is "stickier"—more memorable, and therefore more formative over a longer term.

In order to encourage my students to engage emotionally and achieve this sticky learning, I preface EL with a discussion of the comfort, challenge, and panic zones. For instance, I teach a Community Practice and Research course that meets in a local church that has allocated space for classes. Each week, we attend a free lunch held at the church to observe the event, interact with people from the neighborhood, and experience receiving a community service. The lunch is our primary CEL activity in the course and why I teach the class at this location. Before we go the first time, I ask students to consider what is in their comfort zone as it pertains to attending the lunch. For some, talking to a new person each week is within their comfort zones, but for many students, sitting by themselves or at a table with only their classmates and not eating what is offered is an emotionally safer place. Next, we discuss panic zones. I emphasize that entering one's panic zone is not helpful to anyone: neither the student, their classmates, community members, nor I benefit from or value individuals pushing themselves into a panic zone. We don't need emotional martyrs. Individually, students consider what could cause them to enter their panic zones and how their minds and bodies tell them when they're there.

Finally, I ask students to think about their challenge zones. What actions can they take during lunch that would push them out of their comfort zones yet keep them from panic? Some students decide to sit next to someone they don't know. For others, it's about the food and trying something they didn't prepare and cannot choose. And for a small group of students, entering the room of strangers and taking a seat is a challenge. To engage further would induce the overwhelming emotion of the panic zone. After encouraging students to enter the challenge zone that they have identified (but not disclosed), we go to lunch.

When we enter the large hall in the basement, there are about twelve tables set up with six to ten chairs and place settings. The room typically has three women filling plates of food, two men delivering food and drinks to guests and bussing tables, and ten to twenty people who have come to eat and/or get a haircut, offered at the far end of the room behind a partition. Usually, the crowd reflects the surrounding neighborhood: mostly African-American people with a handful of white people. Most people are over 50 years old, though some are younger, including those who come on their lunch break from local construction sites. Through conversation over the years, I've learned that several are there for the social interaction that they don't often get from living alone, others attend for the excellent food, and some come because of economic necessity.

As an instructor, it is fascinating to observe student behavior on the first day. Some are quickly chatting with someone from the neighborhood that they just met. Other students are observing the room cautiously, but keenly, on their first day. A few students often leave the student "pack" to sit at a table already crowded with neighborhood guests who seem to know the ropes of the community lunch, and a larger group finds seats together, often within proximity to one or two community members. At this point, it is difficult to refrain from assessing students' seating choices or number of words exchanged with those outside of the class as markers of whether students are challenging themselves or not. Yet, if I want students to attend to their own comfort, challenge, and panic zones, which is necessary for learning in this environment, then I must trust them to start where they need to start and watch for growth from there. My challenge zone when teaching includes trusting the process of EL.

For, as I remind students several times during a semester, one's challenge zone moves (Ryan, 2006). As we become comfortable with a previously challenging environment or behavior, it no longer ushers us into our challenge zone. This is growth! To continue learning, then, we need to identify new bounds of our challenge zones. One way I measure success in EL is that where we start should not be where we end. In other words, what challenges us in week 15 should be different from what challenged us in week 1. In addition, one's challenge zone is influenced by other aspects of our emotional lives and therefore fluctuates. I observed this in a student who started the semester by disclosing to me that understanding her own challenge zone regarding the community lunch included acknowledging her experience of an eating disorder. For this student, her behavior toward the food offered (eating some, eating a little, politely refusing when served, not attending the lunch) was highly dependent upon other stressors in her life and her levels of anxiety that week. Her challenge zone changed weekly and in a non-linear fashion, illustrating that learning outcomes in CEL are often different for each student.

In my experience, students readily adopt the language of the challenge zone. One student applied the concept to deciding what to do post graduation:

> As I discerned if I wanted to do a year of service (what program, what placement, what city, etc.) I thought about how I really needed to do something outside of my comfort zone and do something in my challenge zone. And so I did! I surprised myself by choosing to accept a placement on the West Coast because I knew it was outside of my comfort zone. Now having been here for two months, it has been challenging but it has been so good for me too. I'm so glad that when I was going through the process of deciding, I had my challenge zone in mind. (Student C, personal communication, October 21, 2020)

On another occasion, a student was able to articulate that her experience of going door-to-door in a neighborhood was abbreviated because a loose dog pushed her into her panic zone. From our prior conversations, she understood that continuing her work that day was not necessary. The concepts of the zones are accessible and helpful for students.

On course evaluations, students are asked to identify the aspects of courses that are most effective for their learning. For the Community Practice and Research course, students almost always discuss meeting at the community center and attending the community lunches among the most effective pieces of the class. Students' descriptors for this CEL experience have included "super beneficial," "special," and something that a student "loved." One student reflected,

I think being in the challenge zone helped me overcome preconceived notions about people. I thought I knew what kind of people would be coming to the church for lunch, but I was (gladly) wrong and really benefited from conversations with neighbors. Being in the challenge zone does [cause] you to be uncomfortable with your own feelings and I think it really is a place to learn, even if you thought you knew how something was...overall I like the concept of the challenge zone because it pushed me to challenge thoughts and ideas I had in my mind and pushed me to grow and learn, and be okay being a little uncomfortable along the way. (Student B, personal communication, October 16, 2020)

By utilizing CEL, I can facilitate "sticky" learning for students, which is further justified by students' generally positive response to it.

Learning What I Cannot Teach

Along with fostering "sticky" learning, CEL allows students to learn things that I am unable to teach them on my own. As I educate social work students, I am acutely aware of the bounds of my effectiveness due to my privilege as a white, educated, cisgender, Christian person. Since I teach at a private, Catholic, predominately white institution (PWI), my students often share some aspects of my identity and privilege, though there are always some who do not. I am not the right person to teach my students about many aspects of oppression, but it's critical that they—and I—understand how privilege and power operate in the social world, especially from the perspective of people with identities different from theirs. The Council on Social Work Education (2015) established "engaging with diversity and difference in practice" as a core competency for students to master, asserting that social workers "present themselves as learners and engage clients and constituencies as experts of their own experiences" (p. 7). CEL allows me to fulfill this mandate as a social worker myself, model a learning posture for my students, and facilitate education about the social world for all of us.

A specific instance of students learning what I can't teach them occurred as part of a second CEL project in the Community Practice and Research course. Through a collaboration with a local community development organization, students assisted with the organization's work to understand needs and clearly communicate processes and available resources with residents of a local public housing development who are facing displacement due to property renovations.

> Even though I was put in the challenge zone it helped me see the honest reality of what I was learning about in class. It made me more empathetic. One instance that will forever be ingrained in my memory is when a few of us went to [the public housing community] for their neighborhood meeting. I will always remember the residents' faces of feeling hopeless, confused, and angry about the uncertainty of when their home would be demolished. And that is something that cannot be taught in a classroom. (Student A, personal communication, November 8, 2020)

This student's reflection demonstrates the impact of CEL: sustained learning ("will forever be ingrained in my memory") about the social world ("honest reality of what I was learning about in class"), achieved through personal experiences ("something that cannot be taught in a classroom"). As an instructor, I cannot achieve this depth of learning on my own.

A specific instance of students learning what I can't teach them occurred during the loose dog incident described previously. Several students, most of whom were white, described feeling unsafe when going door-to-door in a neighborhood near campus of mostly people who are black. We talked at length about the observations that led to these feelings in our next class. At the end of the semester, our culminating experience was participating in a neighborhood workday to assist elderly homeowners with small maintenance jobs, such as painting and landscaping. Though we were in the same neighborhood in which students had previously felt unsafe, the same students reported feeling comfortable during the workday. Through reflection, some students realized that their perceptions of safety were based on whether they felt racially different from those around them, as they had when going door-to-door, or whether they felt accompanied by a larger group of mostly white people. Through an emotionally engaged experience of racial difference, students were able to explore the concept of a "safe" neighborhood and understand that it sometimes has little to do with crime statistics.

Another example occurred during one of the weekly lunches. One of the hosts facilitated a short program during which one student introduced our class as "from UD." At this, a community member laughed dismissively, which insulted the student speaker as well as a few other students (while still other students were angry with the upset students for being upset). Serendipitously, a lifelong Dayton resident was our guest speaker in the class following this incident. After the student described the experience, our guest said, "Are you familiar with white privilege?" This started an important conversation about the role of the university in the community, differences between the student body and the community residents, and race and class privilege. The discussion was lively because it was in response to an authentic experience in which students were emotionally invested. Though I can talk about privilege with my students and discuss university-community relations any day, CEL produced a more engaged and relevant discussion which is more likely to have contributed to deeper learning.

In spring semesters, I facilitate an Inside-Out Prison Exchange Program (Pompa, 2013) course that's held in a correctional institution. Half of the students are university students ("outside students"), and the other half are experiencing incarceration ("inside students"). It is a unique CEL opportunity for the outside students, given how few of us who have never been incarcerated ever enter a prison, and it's a unique educational opportunity for the inside students, given how few people who have experienced incarceration have access to college courses. The experience teaches numerous things that I cannot teach students without EL. For inside students, many learn for the first time that they can successfully complete a college course, that higher education can be for them. More deeply, inside students are reminded who they are. "This class reminded me of my dignity," one inside student shared at the end of a semester. The availability, structure, and interactions in the class communicate the value and worth of all participants in ways that words alone cannot accomplish. For outside students, the class provides exposure to the carceral system and people—with names, families, and diverse interests—who are experiencing it firsthand. Further, I can think of few better ways to encourage social work students to apply the professional value of dignity and worth of individuals (National Association of Social Workers, 2017) to people who experience incarceration. CEL allows students to deeply learn what I cannot teach them as effectively on my own.

REFLECTION

During the neighborhood workday one spring (described previously) our class was paired with a group of employees from the university. The staff members were so pleased that the students were, in their eyes, "completing a service project" as a requirement of their final exam. "It's so much better [that they're here] than writing another paper!" one staff member told me. The thing is, I assign a lot of papers. Students in my CEL courses write weekly three-page papers that include sections for reflection, and though it can feel like a lot to assess, I keep assigning them every semester. The reflection component is too valuable to their learning to lose.

While some colleagues that I respect tailor their reflection prompts to course content modules, I err on the side of consistency by giving students essentially the same assignment every week, which is an adaptation of the reflection paper assignment from the Inside-Out Prison Exchange Program curriculum (Pompa, 2013). The first section of the assignment asks students to report three observations they made during class that week and a short description of why that observation is meaningful. The observations can come from class sessions or time spent on CEL. The second section is more difficult—an original analysis or integration of the week's readings and course materials. This section is required to be two pages in length, and some students struggle at first to avoid merely summarizing an assigned author. The goal here, however, is for students to make connections among sources. The final section of the paper is for reactions, where students can include their thoughts and feelings from the week. While I find it immensely valuable to understand how students are responding to the course, it is also helpful to students to have a spot to write about their intellectual and emotional experiences so that these don't become the focus of the other sections of the paper. Once students understand the expectations for each section, they usually find a rhythm of jotting down observations during class, noting connections among readings as they go, and taking a breath at the end of the week to understand their reactions.

In my experience, reflection has been key for students to achieve sticky learning through CEL. Through verbal and written reflection, students establish narratives of events, clarify their emotional reactions in response to experiences, and articulate specific things that they've learned. In an academic climate that encourages a frenetic pace through coursework, extracurriculars, work, and social activities, time to reflect during class as well as written reflection assignments permit students the space to remember and evaluate their experience, further imprinting the memory of it and what they learned from it. It has also been helpful to have students review their own written reflections. When I ask students to review their earlier reflection papers, students are often pleased with the growth that they observe. This in itself can be affirming to students, based on their own observations and not words of others that can sometimes seem empty. One student wrote,

> Reflecting on the first reflection paper, this class has helped me be more adaptable in different situations. In my first reflection paper, I wrote, "I was a deer in the headlights and did not know where I should sit." I remember going downstairs to the lunchroom, and being clueless and awkward. Now, I feel silly for thinking partaking in lunch, and sitting with strangers was the hardest thing for me to do at the time. Everyone that I had met through lunch has given me in-depth perspectives of their struggles and dreams that I would have not learned back on campus. In the later reflection papers, I wrote about the conversations that I had with people. It goes to show the growth of being able to communicate and feeling comfortable in discussing sensitive topics. (Student A, personal communication, May 4, 2020)

By recording her reactions and later reviewing them, this student was able to see areas in which she had developed competence and confidence during the semester.

In the same way, reflecting on the value of CEL to my teaching leads me to reaffirm my commitment to it, even though it can be more time consuming and carries with it a greater risk of failure than my courses that do not include CEL. I am reminded that CEL keeps me in my challenge zone as an instructor, since experiences are less predictable than lectures and my lesson plans are more often derailed. Recalling the memories of specific examples of important discussions prompted by CEL and my feelings of accomplishment on those days brings back the knowledge that memory and emotion are tied, so learning is facilitated by emotional engagement. Further, my sense of success came from getting students to confront aspects of the social world and consider challenging concepts in ways that I could not have accomplished without CEL. Reflection further ingrains in me what I have learned, what I know.

Stars in the Sky

Back at camp, the last night of the week was often very emotional for campers. Camp staff would hold candles, make a large circle around all of the campers, and sing a song about remembering the summer when you see stars at night. These days, I don't use the stars to remember what CEL has taught me, and I don't think my students do, either. Instead, I remember specific questions and phrases that have been spoken during important discussions. I remember students engaging in a neighborhood in ways that seemed like too far of a stretch for them during week one. I remember an inside and outside student genuinely laughing together, when a few short months before, both were unsure and a little suspicious of each other. Through these moments, CEL has taught me that CEL is worth it and that there may be no better way to engage students in learning about the social world.

REFERENCES

Council on Social Work Education. (2015). 2015 *educational policy and accreditation standards for baccalaureate and master's social work programs.* https://www.cswe.org/getattachment/Accreditation/Accreditation-Process/2015-EPAS/2015EPAS_Web_FINAL.pdf.aspx

Freire, P. (1993). *Pedagogy of the oppressed* (M. B. Ramos, Trans.; 20th Anniversary ed. ed.). Continuum.

Immordino-Yang, M. H. (2016). Introduction: Why emotions are integral to learning. In M. H. Immordino-Yang (Ed.), *Emotions, learning, and the brain: Exploring the educational implications of affective neuroscience* (pp. 17–24). W.W. Norton.

Nagda, B. A., Gurin, P., & Lopez, G. E. (2003). Transformative pedagogy for democracy and education. *Race, Ethnicity, and Education, 6*(2), 165–191.

National Association of Social Workers. (2017). *Code of ethics.* https://www.socialworkers.org/About/Ethics/Code-of-Ethics/Code-of-Ethics-English

Polk, T. A. (2018). *How stress and emotion affect learning [Video].* The Great Courses.

Pompa, L. (2013). Drawing forth, finding voice, making change: Inside-out learning as transformative pedagogy. In S. W. Davis & B. S. Roswell (Eds.), *Turning teaching inside-out: A pedagogy of transformation for community-based education* (pp. 13–25). Palgrave Macmillan.

Ryan, M. J. (2006). *This year I will…: How to finally change a habit, keep a resolution, or make a dream come true.* Broadway Books.

CHAPTER 3

Desperate Times Call for Experiential Learning: The Evolution of the Community Agency Project

Catherine Lawless Frank

In the fall of 2013, I was asked to teach the undergraduate teacher education course I dreaded the most, *Collaborating with Families, Professionals, and Agencies.* This course is designed to teach intervention specialist/special education teacher candidates the skills to effectively partner with people of diverse backgrounds and has traditionally been taught in a typical classroom style. I never wanted to teach this course and avoid doing so for ten years. I dreaded the thought of lecturing about collaboration. It seemed so insincere and dull. How could 22-year-old students learn to communicate effectively and partner with others in the outside world through a mandatory college lecture class? The available textbooks and resources were of little help and felt superficial and disingenuous to develop the skills to productively work with older, religiously, culturally, and ethnically diverse adults. Before incorporating experiential learning

C. L. Frank (✉)
Teacher Education, University of Dayton, Dayton, OH, USA
e-mail: clawless1@udayton.edu

© The Author(s), under exclusive license to Springer Nature
Switzerland AG 2022
K. Lovett (ed.), *Diverse Pedagogical Approaches to Experiential Learning, Volume II,*
https://doi.org/10.1007/978-3-030-83688-7_3

25

(EL), I dreaded each class (and the course evaluations from my students). I spent hours planning and designing collaborative projects, activities, and case studies to highlight the material, but both the students and I were bored, unmotivated, and disengaged.

It is not that I do not value collaboration or understand the need for teacher education candidates to develop collaborative dispositions. It is a critical and necessary skill for teachers, especially for those in special education, and ensuring candidates can do so is mandated through both state and professional standards. For instance, Standard 6 of Ohio's Standards for the Teaching Profession requires teachers to be able to collaborate and communicate clearly and effectively (Ohio's Educator Standards, 2005). The Council for Exceptional Children, the accrediting body for special education, requires beginning teachers to be proficient at using "theory and elements of effective collaboration" and do so "in culturally responsive ways" (Council for Exceptional Children, 2020). The course, *Collaborating with Families, Professionals, and Agencies*, was designed to ensure candidates meet these accreditation requirements but I struggled to find ways to effectively do so.

According to the Merriam-Webster Online Dictionary (2020), collaboration is "to work jointly with others" and "to cooperate with an agency or instrumentality with which one is not immediately connected." This definition alone made it challenging because the students were already "immediately connected." They are typically fourth-year students who had formed cohorts, support groups, and friendships in their previous three years and multiple classes together. Before the course, the candidates had numerous opportunities to participate in collaborative group and team activities and become "immediately connected." Their prior experiences together made my in-class group activities fall short in developing skills that generalize to working with others who are not immediately connected.

Many students in the course seemed to think they were already proficient at collaboration and that the ability to do so was evident and intuitive. In some respects, in the classroom environment, it was. Collaboration is a goal-oriented process where each individual brings their unique knowledge and expertise to jointly solve a problem or complete a task (Moseley, n.d.). Foundational to successful collaborative groups are developing trusting relationships in and among team members as well as fostering self-awareness and clear communication (Bennett & Gadlin, 2012). Unbeknownst or unconsciously through their three years (and many hours and projects), the students developed the foundations of being a successful collaborative group. Their prior course work and the inclusive environments found in many teacher education classes help build the cohort as a collaborative team and establish primarily respectful, trusting relationships among them. Class projects had a shared vision or goal, but it was often predetermined or set by teacher requirements and expected learning outcomes. Endeavors outside of class, such as those found in sororities, fraternities, sports, and clubs, also contain many of these foundational pieces. While individuals may not initially know one another, they are typically approximately the same age, with comparable degrees of professional development, similar backgrounds, and a predetermined shared vision. The students' belief that they "know how to collaborate" may have been true in the classroom and university environment but often not tested in a diverse unfamiliar situation that required building collaborative relationships, greater self-awareness, and effective communication skills.

The students in this course mirrored the national trends for beginning first-year teachers of being predominantly white, middle-class, Christian, monocultural, and monolingual (Bowles, 2011). They appear to have a seemingly naive view of differing sociocultural realities and limited exposure to working with diverse populations. Expanding our students' collaborative skills is critical, especially given that the population in our nation's schools and surrounding communities is becoming more diverse culturally and economically and less aligned to teacher demographics. As the majority of teachers remain White females, an increasing number of students in k-12 classrooms are of different ethnic and cultural minorities (National Center for Educational Statistics, 2016). These differences often cause a disconnect between the sociocultural realities of teachers and students. It intensifies the need to educate and provide teacher education candidates with authentic experiences that prepare them to implement effective collaborative skills and understand the diverse perspectives and different sociocultural realities of their students.

In the first few years of teaching this class, I tried to provide my students with these necessary skills by following the traditional teaching manner in a university classroom. I devoted hours to developing lectures, finding appropriate resources, and developing activities but nothing seemed to work or engage the students. The content seemed shallow and redundant, and the students and I were bored. I wanted to develop a project that challenged the students and expose them to a more authentic and realistic application of the course content and material but had no idea what to do or how to begin. One day, as fate would have it, at a school event for our children, I complained about the course to a colleague who worked in the university's Leadership in Community program. Unbeknownst to me, she had the resources and provided the motivation for me to revise my course and incorporate EL. With her support and ideas from other colleagues, the Collaborative Agency Project (CAP) began to develop. It ultimately emerged as a semester-long immersion that provided candidates with firsthand experience working in solidarity with community partners. Through the development and implementation of the CAP, the two most glaring lessons I learned were that the collaboration between partners must be voluntary, and clear ongoing communication is essential for project success.

EXPERIENTIAL LEARNING IN TEACHER EDUCATION

The teacher education program provides numerous EL opportunities, called field experiences or labs, for our candidates in k-12 schools. These field experiences are typically tied to a course as an additional requirement or embedded in the course itself. A "lab" requires approximately 20 hours of field experience in schools and is designed to model effective teaching practices and facilitates the class content. Students in the *Collaborating with Families, Professionals, and Agencies* had previously had over 100 hours of these experiences in a variety of K-12 classrooms. They were typically in the first semester of their cumulative EL activity, student teaching. During student teaching, candidates are partnered with a cooperating or mentor teacher to work and learn alongside them in a K-12 classroom aligned to their specific licensure area. In all, candidates spend over 600 hours in EL activities in K-12 public and private schools in both suburban and urban environments. But, they have minimal time or exposure to EL activities in communities and agencies outside the school environment.

The need for pre-service teachers to participate in experiences outside the classroom within diverse communities is well-documented. The demographics of schools are changing with the number of White students remaining relatively steady since 2008 (with a decrease of approximately 1%), while those that are Hispanic, Asian/Pacific Islander, and American Indian/Alaska Native have increased approximately 25%, 36%, and 17%, respectfully. Teachers in the United States continue to be approximately 80% White females whereas 50% of the students are not White and/or not females (National Center for Educational Statistics, 2016). This demographic divergence makes it imperative for teachers to be able to understand not just their own culture but also that of their students (Villegas & Lucas, 2002). A lack of awareness and exposure to different cultures and sociocultural realities between teachers and students often results in misinterpretations and misunderstandings. Facilitating opportunities to learn from and alongside community members before becoming a practicing teacher fosters a greater understanding of the different components of culture and their influence on education. EL opportunities within communities can help to strengthen cultural competencies, and better prepare teachers to confront the biases and cultural misunderstanding that exacerbate the challenges in our nation's schools (Villegas & Lucas, 2002; Marx & Pecina, 2016; Tinkler et al., 2014).

I wanted to develop a collaborative project that fills the void in EL activities in communities and agencies outside the school environment. According to Zeichner, Bowman, and Guillen (2016), these opportunities take three forms based on the lengths and goals of the project. These include *involving, engaging,* and *working in solidarity* with the community. *Involvement* is typically a short-duration school-based interaction designed to help candidates develop the skills to talk to and interact with families and community members. The focus is primarily to allow schools to share information and includes activities such as attending parent-teacher nights, PTA meetings, and homework assignments that include a school-family connection. *Engagement* allows for more participation and sharing of information and includes activities such as home visits, and neighborhood walks led by families or community members. The goal is for candidates to learn from and develop a greater understanding of families and community members. The final approach is *working in solidarity,* which involves sustained engagement within the community in which candidates and community members become co-collaborators and work together toward a shared goal.

While each of the three forms is beneficial, the *working in solidarity* approach seemed to provide the most appropriate framework for aligning the course components and requirements for developing a community-based immersive CAP.

COLLABORATIVE AGENCY PROJECT (CAP)

The Collaborative Agency Project (CAP), a result of the frustration, desperation, and colleague support, is a semester-long project that provides candidates with firsthand experience working in solidarity within the greater Dayton community. In small groups, students worked with community partners (libraries, homeless shelters, children wellness programs, adults with disabilities…), all nonprofits, to develop and implement collaborative projects. Diverse community members from the agencies served as mentors. The CAP allows students to develop collaborative relationships with individuals that are not immediately familiar or connected and are of varying ages, professional knowledge, and backgrounds. It provides students a degree of collaborative relationship building and clear communication that is typically not necessary in a university classroom environment. The mutually beneficial, authentic aspect of the projects enhances engagement in developing and applying the course content and materials. This arrangement allowed students to generalize skills and develop trusting relationships (a key and missing component of in-class collaboration) with people of differing backgrounds and cultures. CAP afforded a genuine platform for the students to meet the Ohio and Council of Exceptional Children Teaching Standards. They were able to "share responsibility" (Ohio's Educator Standards, 2005) as well as use the "theory and elements of effective collaboration" and "in culturally responsive ways" (Council for Exceptional Children, 2020).

Since the course was offered Fall semester, project development began in the late spring and summer with contacting and meeting with nonprofit agencies and Neighborhood Schools Centers to determine their interest. In the beginning, identifying and contacting potential partners was one of the most challenging aspects for me. I found it intimidating and relied on support from the university's Fitz Center for Leadership in Community center. The process became much easier once I became more experienced and comfortable with identifying potential partners and initiating contact. Ultimately, I found that I enjoyed exploring the community to identify partners and that most agencies were willing and happy to work with us. Sometimes though it was challenging to determine an appropriate project, partnerships just did not work out.

Prior to the beginning of the course, I met with the agencies to brainstorm ideas based on course requirements, the agency's needs, and the projects' size and scope. Ultimately, about five agencies and Neighborhood

School Centers were recruited each semester, and an agency contact person was designated. Some partnerships remained consistent for multiple years (Dayton Metro Libraries, United Rehabilitation Services, Safe Kids) while new ones were developed annually based on their availability and needs.

At the beginning of the semester, students were provided a choice in the CAP. They were given an overview of each project and community partner and then ranked their preferences (1–5 with one being most interested). Groups of three to five students were formed based on these rankings. Candidates then met in their groups to complete an agency background (history, mission, vision statement...) and group information form. This form has been revised throughout the years to better ensure students have appropriate background knowledge and to develop group norms, share relevant contact information, and plan for the initial meeting with the agency. Group member roles were determined (communications director, meeting leader, note-taker, coordinator...), and the designated communication director connected the agency and arranged the initial meeting. See Table 3.1: Beginning Organizational Structure for an overview of the structure for the beginning of the CAP projects.

During this initial in-person meeting, the students and agency collaborated to complete a CAP planning guide. Since the students in the course were studying to become Intervention Specialist/Special Education teachers, the project's planning guide's structure mimicked the collaborative design process of an Individual Education Program (IEP) (see Table 3.2:

Table 3.1 Beginning Organizational Structure

CAP structure for the beginning of the projects
1. Students rank project preferences
2. Groups formed based on preferences
3. Groups complete agency background and group information form
4. Contact with agency initiated by group and first meeting arranged
5. CAP planning guide completed in collaboration with agency representative to determine the projects
    (a) Current status
    (b) Goal
    (c) Steps necessary to complete the goal
    (d) Available resources
    (e) Potential barriers
    (f) Measurements for success
    (g) Means of identifying and reporting concerns

Table 3.2   Comparison of IEP and CAP

	Individualized education program	*Collaborative agency project planning guide*
Initial status/ present levels	The student's baseline or present levels of academic achievement and functional performance	The project's starting point or the current status of the CAP project before UD student involvement
Goal	Annual goal—what the student should realistically be able to know or do within a calendar year	Project goal—what the students and agency realistically plan to accomplish within the project duration
Objectives	Necessary steps to help the student reach their goal	Necessary action steps to help the students and agency reach their goal

Comparison of IEP and CAP). The development of an IEP involves parents, teachers, and administrators working together to determine a student with a disability's yearly educational program in academic and behavioral areas (reading fluency, comprehension, speech, and language development). It is a written document that, in part, details the student's present levels of performance (how they are doing now) and corresponding goals and objectives for the year. Learning to develop, write, and implement an IEP collaboratively is a significant requirement for special education fourth-year candidates when most of them are taking this course. Using a similar development process in CAP reinforced this collaborative IEP process.

The CAP planning guide was essentially an IEP for the project and reinforced the need for clear communication as a foundational aspect of collaboration (Bennett & Gadlin, 2012). It established a framework for the direction and desired outcome along with the necessary steps and available resources. During the initial meeting the students and agencies completed the form to determine the scope and sequence of the project. The intent of the guide was to develop a clear specific goal and plan for the project. Some groups used the guide to develop structure (e.g., develop three social stories on how to find materials and check out a book for three different libraries), while others were more vague (to better integrate adults with disabilities into the community). Plans without a specific goal or structure were susceptible to more challenges (such as confusion about what the students were supposed to be doing or different ideas about the direction of the project). In class, I stressed the need for a clear goal and structure but did not feel comfortable intervening or revising a plan developed by an outside agency and adult students. This was ultimately their project. I wanted them to problem-solve, take responsibility, and develop collaborative partnerships without my initial interference.

CAP planning guides that were initially vague, lacked structure and/or an explicit purpose, were successful if the students and agency mentor maintained clear ongoing communication. While this is essential in all collaborative endeavors, it was even more so when the specific project components are not well-defined. The ongoing communication allowed the students and agency mentor to restructure and redefine the plan as needed. For instance, the project that had an initial goal of better integrating adults with disabilities into the community was later clarified to include specific components that the students were then able to implement (work with high school students with disabilities to identify potential employment opportunities of interest). The ongoing communication, while not always consistent, allowed the group to clarify expectations and the nature and structure of the project. This CAP faced challenges but the students were able to overcome them with perseverance and clear communication.

The course itself met twice a week, Mondays and Wednesdays. On Mondays, the class was held in-person to cover course content. Wednesdays were dedicated to working on the CAP. This provided an opportunity for the CAP to serve as a framework and reference point for instruction and course content (developing goals and agendas for meeting, using clarifying language, addressing concerns...). Students were asked to reflect and discuss in class the ties between the curriculum and projects. For example, a potential barrier to collaboration is differing degrees of professional knowledge (Richards et al., 2016). This barrier was a relevant concern for the CAP as college students were partnered with adult professionals. For instance, the professional knowledge of an Adult Service Coordinator at a rehabilitation center or a Children's Services Librarian is different from that of a teacher education college student or a university professor. All parties have valuable knowledge and insight but may hold different priorities, knowledge bases, and beliefs which challenge the collaborative process. Identifying this concern and reflecting on it helped the students brainstorm ways to overcome this barrier and promoted self-awareness and strengthened group communication and cohesion.

Students completed status reports and peer- and self-evaluation forms at both the midterm and the final. Both reports documented progress,

Table 3.3   Final project requirements

Collaborative Agency Project Presentation Guidelines
For your final, you will need to develop a visual (e.g., PowerPoint, trifold) and oral
presentation that addresses the following information:
_____Background information about your agency/school
_____Background information and purpose of your project
_____Status of the project before you started
_____Observable, measurable goal(s) for this project
_____Three to five action steps/objectives used to help reach the goal(s)
_____Resources available
_____Project's successes
_____Project's challenges
_____Was the original goal accomplished? Why or why not?
_____What still needs to be accomplished or completed?
_____Were any changes made to the scope or nature of the project? If so, what and why?
_____What was the role of each group member?
_____What changes your group could have made to make the project more successful?
_____Identify three things your group as a whole learn from this project?

achievements, and challenges. At midterm, I met with the student to debrief and discuss any issues and concerns. While I was always available, the midterm allowed me to provide more specific guidance (typically on ways to maintain communication or identify potential resources). It also gave the student enough time remaining in the semester to make any necessary adjustments. The final also required an oral class presentation with a reflection and an overview of the CAP. See Table 3.3: Final Project Requirements for the final project requirements.

Individually students reflected on their primary takeaways and completed peer- and self-evaluations that addressed individual contributions. Both the reflection questions and the peer- and self-evaluation were designed to increase accountability and facilitated self-awareness, both key components in effective collaborative groups (Bennett & Gadlin, 2012).

LESSONS LEARNED FROM FACULTY

The two most glaring lessons I learned about developing and implementing EL projects are that the collaboration must be voluntary, and clear ongoing communication is essential for the projects to be successful (accomplish their stated goal). When individuals are provided a choice, their motivation and desire to work jointly tend to be higher (Richards et al., 2016). For the students, participating in the CAP was not voluntary. Choices were embedded throughout the process (assignments based on student choices and interest, choice of roles within the group, a voice in determining the goal, structure, and process) to provide ownership and compensate for the project's mandated aspect. Receiving credit and a grade was also an incentive for the students, but as in most group projects, the work itself was not always evenly divided. Some students were more diligent than others, hence the implementation of the peer- and self-evaluation forms. Still, as a whole, the students were dedicated, committed, and rose to the occasion. When projects were not successful in meeting their established goal, it was rarely, if ever, primarily due to the students.

The issue involving choice arose when the agency mentor was assigned to jointly work with the students rather than volunteering to do so. When a colleague or supervisor "volunteered" another person to participate, the chances of developing a successful collaborative partnership seemed to diminish significantly. There tended to be a high probability that the project would fail to meet the designated goal in those instances. This was true even if the CAP goal directly benefited the third party. While the exact reason for the breakdown is unclear, schedule availability and flexibility seemed to be part of the issue. For instance, a CAP project designed to build and develop a resource library to support a case worker's efforts at a homeless shelter was initiated by a colleague and failed to meet its designated goal. The library was to be housed in the shelter, and the original plan was for students to design the physical layout, research and recommend items to purchase, and develop a borrowing procedure for checking out and returning objects. To make the project happen, a partnership was necessary with the caseworker (rather than the initiating colleague) who did not appear to have the time, energy, desire, or schedule flexibility to work with the students even though the project would benefit them and their clients. The students ultimately served more in the role of office assistant (making copies and putting them in a binder) rather than developing a resource library. This breakdown tended to be the case in most CAPs in which a third party was "volunteered" to collaborate and include an after-school program for elementary students, expanding a school community garden and developing and facilitating activities with high school English language learners. These projects tended to experience issues with ongoing communication and often established an ambiguous initial goal at the planning meeting. These combined factors usually resulted in a failure to successfully complete the CAP (but served as a great lesson in the essential components for collaboration).

The necessity for clear and ongoing communication by all parties was the second major lesson learned. This communication began before the start of the semester between the agency and myself and included in-person meetings with detailed information about the course, project, and student expectations. The students initiated contact with their agency on the first day of the project and arranged in-person meetings to complete the initial planning guide. Midterm checks and ongoing in-class discussions were designed to help support and encourage the students with regular and ongoing communication among each other and with the agency mentor. The projects that develop a clear plan (through the use of the planning guide) and maintained ongoing communication between the students and agency mentor tended to be the most successful. For example, the goal and planning guide for a CAP with the Dayton Metro Libraries stated that they would be "creating social stories for two libraries," identified the specific libraries and contact person. Both librarians volunteered to collaborate with the students and maintained ongoing communication throughout. The project accomplished the goal and resulted in specific social stories on how to navigate and use each individual library. Constant communication is crucial. CAPs with a vague initial planning guide could be successful with ongoing discussions. When communication breaks down, the chances for success were slim, even if the initial goal and planning guide were well-defined. Constant communication is a decisive factor in successful collaboration (Bennett & Gadlin, 2012).

Lessons Learned from Students

While learning to collaborate is an ongoing process, the CAP gave students an opportunity to develop a better understanding of what is required to make it successful. It provided an authentic experience outside the students' typical frame of reference to work jointly with an agency with which they were not immediately connected. The experience allowed students to work in solidarity with diverse community members to refine and improve their collaborative skills. The students' final reflections indicated that through the development and implementation of the CAP, they learned the importance of ongoing communication, building relationships, and implementing structure as foundational necessities of effective collaboration (Moseley, n.d.; Bennett & Gadlin, 2012).

Overwhelmingly, final reflections indicated that students understood the need for clear communication and the importance of sharing their thoughts, visions, and goals for the project frequently (Bennett & Gadlin, 2012). They emphasized the need for strong communication in the beginning to establish a goal and framework and that it could not stop after the first few meetings. Communication needed to be ongoing and maintained throughout the semester. While this was typically not a large challenge within the student groups, it became one in some circumstances with the agency mentor. At times groups struggled with maintaining communication with the agency and feeling like a "pest" when trying to do so. This became a balance for some groups as they felt vested in the project yet struggled to receive input from the agency mentor. Reflections indicated that many groups felt that their projects could have been more successful with greater communication and that "communication can really make or break a project."

Students also noticed the difference in collaborating with those to whom they had not previously developed a relationship and were therefore not immediately connected. This difference was observed among both student groups and the outside agency. Peers who had previously worked together were seen as great at communicating with each other while unfamiliar peers tended to not participate as often. This dynamic improved as group members developed relationships and got to know each other. More significant challenges were found in developing professional relationships with the agency mentor. Students reported that working with group members in class was a lot easier and more comfortable than with the mentor. They identified this "real experience" as more challenging with differing realities, conflicting schedules and off campus meetings. Developing this relationship required students to devote more time and energy and to be more flexible and open. At times understanding differing perspectives and finding a common ground was challenging, and "building rapport with the people you are working with" was seen as some of the project's most significant takeaways.

Students also identified the project's structure as beneficial to the overall experience, especially in terms of assigning roles and conducting midterm peer- and self-evaluations. Having each group determine individual student's roles tended to help the process run smoothly. It allowed for clear communication of expectations and held all group members accountable for their work. The midterm gave them a chance to reflect, evaluate, and address concerns. Providing this opportunity facilitated self-awareness, responsibility, and accountability according to the students.

The development of the CAP projects also was not always easy or smooth. There was a steep learning curve in the beginning, and at times, projects failed to meet their established goal. Throughout these projects though students and agency mentors collaborated to:

- Write social stories and develop visual support for multiple libraries and a bookmobile
- Develop and facilitate a book club for adults with disabilities
- Work with an immigration integration center to plan, coordinate, and facilitate a panel discussion by local immigrants for the university community
- Assess adults with disabilities to determine their interest, job, and community awareness
- Create activities, incentives, and resources to promote attendance at area elementary schools
- Produce a photovoice project and webpage to help address safety concerns near area schools
- Design lessons to enhance accessibility of exhibits for a local museum
- Conduct research on safe walks to school as part of an injury prevention program
- Generate lessons to promote playing for children

All of the CAPs, whether or not they met their established goal, provided students with an EL projected outside their typical frame of reference. They succeeded in teaching and reinforcing the needed course content far better than through a traditional classroom format. Students reflected on how much they learned and stated that it was "the most enjoyable group project experience that (they) have had in a long time." Success was attributed to their ability to communicate, be productive, and provide differing perspectives.

Collaboration is easy when everything works well, but challenges make the content more relevant and provide a more robust backdrop for self-awareness and reflection. As one student put it, "I learned from this project that collaboration is something that in theory sounds very easy but (is more challenging) when actually executing it with people who have differing personalities and visions." The learning and professional growth for both my students and myself far exceeded my expectations in meeting the course goals. It brought new enthusiasm and purpose to class content and better provided my students with the skills and disposition to develop partnerships with the communities and families they will be impacting as teacher educators.

REFERENCES

Bennett, M. L., & Gadlin, H. (2012). Collaboration and team science. *Journal of Investigative Medicine, 60,* 768–775. https://doi.org/10.2310/JIM.0b013e318250871d

Bowles, F. A. (2011). Transformation – More than meets the eye: Teacher candidates' journeys to cultural competence. *Action in Teacher Education, 33,* 542–559.

Council for Exceptional Children. (2020). *Initial preparation standards.* Council for Exceptional Children. https://exceptionalchildren.org/standards/initial-special-education-preparation-standards

Marx, D., & Pecina, U. (2016). Community: The missing piece in preparing teacher candidates for future urban classrooms. *Action in Teacher Education, 38*(4), 344–357.

Merriam-Webster Dictionary. (2020). *Collaborate.* https://www.merriam-webster.com/dictionary/collaborate

Moseley, C. (n.d.). *Collaboration vs cooperation: What's the difference?* Jostle. Retrieved from https://blog.jostle.me/blog/collaboration-vs-cooperation

National Center for Educational Statistics. (2016). http://nces.ed.gov/programs/digest/d14/tables/dt14_209.10.asp?current=yes

Ohio's Educator Standards. (2005). Retrieved December 7, 2020, from http://education.ohio.gov/Topics/Teaching/Educator-Equity/Ohio-s-Educator-Standards

Richards, S., Lawless Frank, C., Sableski, M., & Arnold, J. (2016). *Collaboration among professionals, students, families and communities: Effective teaming for student learning.* Routledge.

Tinkler, A., Tinkler, B., Gerstl-Pepin, C., & Mugisha, V. M. (2014). The promise of a community-based, participatory approach to service-learning in teacher education. *Journal of Higher Education Outreach and Engagement, 18*(3), 209–232.

Villegas, A., & Lucas, T. (2002). Preparing culturally responsive teachers: Rethinking the curriculum. *Journal of Teacher Education, 53*(1), 20–32.

Zeichner, K., Bowman, M., Guillen, L., & Napolitan, K. (2016). Engaging and working in solidarity with local communities in preparing the teachers of their children. *Journal of Teacher Education, 67*(4), 277–290. https://doi.org/10.1177/0022487116660623

Human Rights Education Through Experiential Learning

Shelley Inglis

In December 2011, the United Nations General Assembly adopted the United Nations Declaration on Human Rights Education and Training (UNDHRET). The Declaration states that "human rights education and training provides persons with knowledge, skills and understanding and develops their attitudes and behaviours to empower them to contribute to the building and promotion of a universal culture of human rights" (A/HRC/42/23 General Assembly 26 July 2019).

This chapter focuses on the role that the Human Rights Center (HRC) at the University of Dayton (UD) plays in human rights education through experiential learning (EL). While traditional academic programs focus on knowledge about human rights, EL contributes to knowledge and skills *about* human rights as well as learning *through* and *for* human rights in practice. Through its various projects and programs, the HRC thus contributes to the World Programme for Human Rights Education focused

S. Inglis (✉)
Human Rights Center, University of Dayton, Dayton, OH, USA
e-mail: singlis1@udayton.edu

K. Lovett (ed.), *Diverse Pedagogical Approaches to Experiential Learning, Volume II*,
https://doi.org/10.1007/978-3-030-83688-7_4

on youth in all dimensions of human rights and to Sustainable Development Goal 4 on global citizenship education in furtherance of contemporary universal agendas.

HUMAN RIGHTS EDUCATION

Human rights education has been a focus of the United Nations since 2004 when it proclaimed the World Programme for Human Rights Education (2005-ongoing) to advance the implementation of human rights education programs in all sectors (A/59/113 General Assembly 10 December 2004).

Now in its fourth phase (2020–2024), the World Programme focuses on youth, with special emphasis on education and training in equality, human rights and non-discrimination, and inclusion and respect for diversity with the aim of building inclusive and peaceful societies (A/ HRC/42/23 General Assembly 26 July 2019).

This emphasis aligns with the 2030 Agenda for Sustainable Development and specifically with target 4.7 of the Sustainable Development Goals (SDGs) which requires states to "ensure all learners acquire knowledge and skills needed to promote sustainable development, including among others through education for sustainable development and sustainable lifestyles, human rights, gender equality, promotion of a culture of peace and non-violence, global citizenship, and appreciation of cultural diversity and of culture's contribution to sustainable development" (A/RES/70/1 General Assembly 21 October 2015).

Human rights education (HRE) is a lifelong process which involves the following:

(a) Education about human rights, which includes providing knowledge and understanding of human rights norms and principles, the values that underpin them and the mechanisms for their protection;
(b) Education through human rights, which includes learning and teaching in a way that respects the rights of both educators and learners;
(c) Education for human rights, which includes empowering persons to enjoy and exercise their rights and to respect and uphold the rights of others. (A/HRC/RES/16/1 General Assembly 8 April 2011)

In the process of education, individuals gain knowledge about and skills to execute human rights, and attitudes, values and beliefs that uphold human rights. As a form of empowerment, they also learn specific behaviors involved in taking action to defend one's own human rights and advocate for the rights of everyone. Thus, HRE requires a holistic approach that incorporates learning that relates to the intellectual or cognitive, social-emotional or affective, and agency or empowerment dimensions of a young person. It contributes to the development or formation of not one part, but rather the whole of the individual.

Building on this, the approach to HRE outlined in this chapter seeks to move beyond the individual to *social transformation*—affecting social action and change more broadly in the world, in addition to the impact on the individual students. The HRE provided by the HRC should be considered a form of *transformative learning*. As in HRE practice, it seeks to provide critical reflection or "conscientization" which stems from a learner-centered environment that promotes autonomy and agency, and encourages self-reflection on positionality and building intercultural competencies. That process is embedded in participation in human rights advocacy with the aim of social change (Transformative Learning and Human Rights Education: Taking a Closer Look, Tibbitts, 2005).

There are multiple sources of guidance on the learning outcomes in the context of education *through* and *for* human rights. In her book, *Human Rights Education*, Sarita Jo Cargas provides a theory of critical pedagogy for HRE and useful guidance on the leading sources which are applicable to educating at the tertiary level. Those that are particularly relevant in the context of this chapter include the following:

From the UNDHRET:

- Providing persons with knowledge, skills, and understanding and developing their attitudes and behaviors, to empower them to contribute to the building and promotion of a universal culture of human rights (Article 2);
- Pursuing the effective realization of all human rights and promoting tolerance, nondiscrimination, and equality;
- Contributing to the prevention of human rights violations and abuses and to the combating and eradication of all forms of discrimination, racism, stereotyping, and incitement to hatred, and the harmful attitudes and prejudices that underlie them (Article 4).

From Nancy Flowers, *HRE Handbook* (Flowers, 2000):

- Promotion of personal enrichment, self-esteem, and respect;
- Empowerment of participants to define what they want to know and to seek information for themselves;

- Encouragement of behavioral and attitudinal change;
- Emphasis on skill-building and practical application of learning;
- Active engagement of all participants in their own learning and a minimum of passive listening;
- Encouragement of nonhierarchical, democratic, collaborative learning environments;
- Respect for the experience of participants and recognition of a variety of points of view;
- Encouragement of reflection, analysis, and critical thinking;
- Engagement of subjective and emotional responses as well as cognitive learning.

THE HUMAN RIGHTS CENTER

UD is one of only a handful of higher education institutions with a human rights center that services undergraduate, as well as graduate and law students, in the United States (US). It is the only university in the state of Ohio, which is the seventh most populated state in the US, with a human rights footprint. The HRC benefits from a cadre of students with knowledge of human rights and development cultivated by long-standing international studies and human rights studies programs, which provide majors and minors in the substantive theory and knowledge of human rights and international relations. The human rights studies program at the University of Dayton is one of the first ever, having been established over 20 years ago in 1998. There are still only eight such programs in the US today.

The HRC's mission focuses on education, dialogue, and research for and about human rights advocacy. Through its focus on advocacy, it aims to contribute to the understanding and improvement of the practice of human rights—referred to at the University of Dayton in the context of social practice—in other words, the ways in which human rights are realized in the lives and living experience of human beings. For this reason, the HRC seeks to bridge the divide between academics and practitioners, as well as theory and practice in order to enhance human rights advocacy. The HRC consists of faculty, staff, graduate, and undergraduate students who contribute to the work of the HRC in various ways.

For youth at the university level, the gap between theory and practice in human rights can be wide. In its most basic definition, EL is the use of active methods of learning by educators to enhance learning outcomes. In much of the literature, EL is also defined by learning through direct experience outside the classroom in a real-world setting, which involves intentional reflection. In this chapter, EL is used in both the sense of an active learning process as well as the actualization of that process through direct experience in a real-world setting (Teaching for Experiential Learning: Five Approaches that Work, Wurdinger & Carlson, 2010). In the context of this chapter, EL is intrinsic to a comprehensive understanding of HRE, which includes the multiple aims of learning *about*, *through*, and *for* human rights.

EL plays a key role in providing meaningful opportunities to engage in practice and the production of human rights advocacy. Practice and production are essential for bridging what is called "the knowing–doing gap." Practice involves skills-based development that includes learning by breaking down skills into constituent activities, while production is considered the process of experimenting with the application of knowledge in realistic situations (Teaching Human Rights at the Tertiary Level: Addressing the 'Knowing –Doing Gap' through a Role-Based Simulation Approach, Banki et al., 2014). Both the international studies and the human rights studies programs at UD require majors to accrue three credit hours in EL.

Human Rights Advocacy

As a multidisciplinary, undergraduate, and graduate institution, the HRC uses a broad and comprehensive definition of advocacy that extends beyond traditional methods. Traditional human rights advocacy is case-based, grounded on research or investigations to prove that individuals or groups of individuals have been subject to human rights violations. It consists of legal cases in domestic courts or international bodies against governments or sometimes non-state actors like corporations, undertaken by organizations such as the American Civil Liberties Union or the Center for Constitutional Rights. In addition, it involves monitoring and reporting of multiple cases or systemic violations with the aim of publicly naming and shaming governments and advocating for specific international action, exemplified by the work of classic human rights organizations like Human Rights Watch and Amnesty International. Amnesty International is built on an activist campaign model that harnesses its membership organizations based in countries around the world to engage in letter writing and other pressure tactics that promote targeted human rights outcomes, such as the release of political prisoners or adoption of new legislation by governments.

Due to its foundation in social practice, the HRC draws on these traditions but embraces an expansive understanding of what constitutes human rights advocacy in order to both prevent and respond to violations through systemic transformation. It is grounded on the moral and philosophical, political and social, as well as legal origins (Pragmatism and Multidimensionality in Human Rights Advocacy, Human Rights Quarterly Volume 40, Number 3, Sharp, 2018). In line with this foundation, the HRC does not view human rights as a separate agenda solely, but rather as an essential element of other global aims, such as peace and security, democracy and the rule of law, sustainable development, and humanitarian action. In this regard, human rights advocacy can contribute meaningfully to social change or action directly in these domains by ensuring a human rights-based approach which advances outcomes in line with human rights norms and standards.

For the purposes of this chapter, the HRC's approach to advocacy can be classified into six spheres which are interrelated and encompass a range of techniques, methods, tools, and approaches, including research which is cross-cutting. This classification draws on the work of Fuyuki Kurasawa who describes five "modes of human rights practice" in his book *The Work of Global Justice* (Kurasawa, 2007).

1. *Witnessing*: e.g., storytelling, imagery, artistic expression, investigating, interviewing, monitoring, truth telling, memorials, commemorations.
2. *Defending*: e.g., allyship, rapid response, law enforcement, courts, tribunals, treaty body representation, protective measures, shelters.
3. *Campaigning*: e.g., awareness-raising, teaching, communications and social media, narratives, curricula, letter-writing, protesting and demonstrating, boycotting.
4. *Connecting*: e.g., convening, coalition-building, coordination, community organizing, dialoguing, conferencing.
5. *Designing*: e.g., crafting participatory methods, tech tools, innovations, mapping and modeling, rights-based programming.
6. *Institutionalization & codification*: e.g., evidence-based policy-making, legislating, expert testimony or advisory functions, norm formulation, authoritative reporting, budgetary allocations, service programming.

Finally, the HRC is also grounded in a critical pedagogy. It trains a critical eye on the trends in advocacy and assessment of effectiveness, with academic research that seeks to unpack and also critique popular transnational advocacy methods and approaches. (e.g., Pruce, 2019 The Mass Appeal of Human Rights; The Elite Politics of Media Advocacy in Human Rights, Senior Researcher Budabin & Pruce, 2018).

HIGH-IMPACT PROGRAMS

The HRC implements projects which result in high-impact EL for students, consisting of education *about*, *through*, and *for* human rights advocacy. In addition to the high-impact programs outlined here, the HRC engages students in learning through a wide range of its work, including in communications and social media, marketing and design, community-based, participatory research and mapping, partnerships and collaborations with other entities, campus and community events planning, awareness-raising, dialogue facilitation, and more. It also provides students with more traditional internship opportunities to work directly with its partners of human rights, development, and peacebuilding organizations.

The high-impact programs of the HRC comprise four core components that are prevalent in various degrees: (1) curricular (credit-bearing) courses with academic content, (2) travel and immersive learning outside of the campus community in a real-world setting, (3) finalization of products which promote human rights advocacy in the "real world," that is, beyond the classroom or campus setting, and (4) collaborative, reciprocal partnerships with a human rights, development, peace or humanitarian non-governmental or civic organization.

Through these programs, students at the undergraduate and graduate level develop knowledge and skills, and attitudes and behaviors by "doing" human rights advocacy. Each of these programs demands that students reflect on and interrogate their positionality in relation to power and privilege as a central element of learning *through* human rights. In these experiences, students confront issues of racial discrimination, gender inequality, poverty and socio-economic inequities within and between countries, stereotyping and incitement to hatred, as well as the harmful attitudes, prejudices, and misinformation that pervade most societies and create the foundation for human rights violations. This is an extremely critical and often-fraught process for students at the UD, a predominantly white, private Marianist Catholic institution in the Midwest of the US. As transformational as they are, many of the students from all these high-impact programs go on to professional careers related to human rights, development, peace, or humanitarian services.

Each of these programs is coordinated and overseen by a faculty or staff member associated with the HRC. The impact on students described here comes from observations and discussions, not systematic data collection, assessment, and evaluation methods (Table 4.1).

THE MORAL COURAGE PROJECT

The Moral Courage Project (MCP) exemplifies this approach. It is a collaboration between the HRC and *PROOF: Media for Social Justice*, a non-governmental organization (NGO) based in New York City that envisions a world full of upstanders. The experience focuses on human rights violations and the voices of those who stand up in the face of crises in the US. So far, it has explored the racial justice movement in Ferguson, Missouri (Ferguson Voices), the treatment of migrants and refugees on the US-Mexico border (America the Borderland) and the right to access clean water in multiple locations, including Flint and Detroit, Michigan, and Appalachia (Poison & Power).

The MCP requires students to participate in a preparatory course, where they learn about the specific human rights violation being studied in the context of its location, as well as skills in interviewing and engagement with human rights upstanders or defenders. It takes students to the location or epi-center of that human rights crisis, where students interview upstanders and participate in community events. Finally, under the supervision and support of faculty, students create a multimedia exhibit that tells the stories of these upstanders, including building a website, producing a podcast, drafting a 'zine', and designing a photo exhibit. Students earn academic credit for these courses. Most recently, the MCP has engaged students in Teacher Education in the formulation of a high school curriculum using the digital materials from the multi-media exhibit, Ferguson Voices, in order to promote the sharing of identities, experiences, and biases by youth in educational settings. Each of the programs outlined in this chapter could serve as a case study in and of themselves. The MCP is the subject of an in-depth review by the faculty that teach and coordinate the project (Florea-Hudson & Pruce, 2020).

Table 4.1 UD HRC high-impact EL programming for human rights education

Program	Advocacy sphere	About HR (knowledge, theory, content)	Through HR (attitudes, values, perspectives)	For HR (skills, behaviors, capacities)
Moral Courage Project (MCP) (documenting the voices and stories of upstanders in the US)	Witnessing (storytelling, narratives about defending, imagery) Campaigning (awareness-raising, education)	Human rights violations in the US (racial discrimination, migration/refugees, economic, social and cultural rights) Community organizing/defending Marginalized voice & agency	Power and privilege in the US context Intersectionality Team work Trauma-informed engagement	Interviewing, designing websites, drafting narratives and themes, producing podcasts, public & multi-media communications, curriculum formulation/lesson planning
Malawi Practicum (research for rights-based local development in Malawi)	Witnessing (interviewing) Designing (research for rights-based programming)	Sustainable development, rights-based approaches to education and local community engagement Southern Africa, Malawi (culture, language, tradition)	Power and privilege in global colonial & racialized inequities, global citizenship Gender inequalities Inter-cultural-linguistic teamwork Personal agency	Interviewing, data collection & analysis, drafting and writing skills, formulation of recommendations for rights-based programming Intercultural competencies, Local development program management, donor/public writing and communications
Abolition Ohio (AO) (coalition to prevent and respond to human trafficking in the Miami Valley, Ohio)	Convening (coalition building, coordination of response), Campaigning (awareness and training) Institutionalization/codification (policy and legal)	Anti-trafficking, forced labor, law enforcement, prosecution and social services, sexual exploitation & abuse Mis-disinformation State and local policy/regulatory/lawmaking	Power & privilege in localized poverty, crime, racial inequities, gender inequalities Long-term local community relationship-building	Public speaking/presenting, teaching & awareness-raising, meeting organizing, public communications, community dialogue facilitation, evidence-based policy/lawmaking

The MCP is an innovative approach to witnessing which engages students in interviewing, storytelling, and the production of imagery of human rights defenders. It requires students to develop questions, engage in empathic listening while interviewing those impacted by human rights violations, and craft others' stories filtered through the students' own perspectives, all of which involves using their judgment and making decisions. The practical skills involved in the production of MCP exhibits are numerous consisting of interviewing, photography, website design and building, drafting of content and execution for podcasts and zines, communications content and social media, and public speaking and narration. With its focus on a broader public awareness-raising and curricular formulation, the MCP engages students in critical aspects of campaigning. Education students develop lesson plans, identifying learning objectives and integrating MCP digital content into various classroom-based active learning activities. Grappling with difficult subject matter grounded in local human rights situations, such as racial injustice, migrants' rights, or the lack of clean water, the students cultivate various skills and knowledge *for* human rights which bring to the forefront the perspectives and advocacy stories of those impacted and taking positive action.

In terms of learning *through* human rights, these students are immersed in a local community or communities for an intensive period, identifying and exploring the trauma and pain of that community, the devastating impact of violations on lives and relationships, and also the individual stories of resilience and commitment. As they develop relationships with individuals, community leaders and advocates, students also formulate strong bonds within their cohort and often gain personal insight by making profound connections with their own family or community origin stories.

THE MALAWI HUMAN RIGHTS AND DEVELOPMENT PRACTICUM

At the international level, the Malawi Research Practicum and the Malawi Graduate Fellowship train future human rights advocates through applied research and working with the community on critical human rights and development issues. Undertaken in partnership with the Malawi-based NGO Determined to Develop (D2D), this project draws on transdisciplinary research and applied participatory international development insights to enable students from across the university, including Teacher Education—School of Education and Health Sciences and ETHOS

Center—School of Engineering, to meaningfully participate in development and human rights work on a global scale. The mission of D2D is to empower, through education, the people of Chilumba, Malawi, to become agents of development for their families, communities, country, and world. The Malawi Research Practicum for undergraduates consists of two curricular courses, one in the Spring preceding travel to Malawi and one on return from the country in the Fall semester, taught by a faculty member or staff. The Spring semester prepares students with learning on international development practice in Africa, the country of Malawi and issues of concern in rights-based development in Malawi which prepares them for undertaking their research. Classes involve engaging with graduate and undergraduate students who have taken the Practicum, conducting a literature review on their research topic, developing intercultural competencies, and exploring relevant scholarship in relation to development, rights-based approaches, and research methodologies.

During the summer, students spend nine weeks involved in applied community-oriented research at D2D's base in Chilumba, Malawi, which lies in the north of the country on Lake Malawi. The practicum gives undergraduate students the opportunity to gain graduate-level research and fieldwork experience on topic areas relevant to the development and human rights issues impacting Malawi. During their time, the UD students are partnered with students from Livingstonia University in Malawi, with the Malawian students also acting as translators. As a team, they conduct research projects, interviewing community members and conducting site visits, based on community-identified needs and supported by D2D staff. On their return during their Fall semester, the UD students engage in reflection on their intercultural experience and finalize these research projects into papers which provide recommendations to D2D for programming, based on analysis of their data and findings. Much of the data and research produced by the students can be tracked to the evaluation and development of new programs and interventions by D2D. UD provides full travel support and program fees, including living expenses for all selected students. Students earn academic credit for the program.

In 2017, the Malawi Practicum was expanded to offer a graduate-level experience. The Malawi Graduate Fellowship is a program designed to support a UD recent graduate or graduating senior with a yearlong field experience working as a Program Officer for D2D. The role of the Program Officer encompasses communications, donor outreach through social media and otherwise, curriculum development, and assisting with the implementation of a variety of education projects in the Chilumba area, such as school sponsorships, female empowerment initiatives, extended learning opportunities for youth, and school partnerships. In addition, the Graduate Fellow plays an important role in supporting the undergraduate Malawi Research Practicum during the research period in Malawi.

Upon completion of the program, the student receives a graduate assistantship at the HRC and a scholarship to enroll and pursue a Master's program at the UD. During the Graduate Assistantship, the student supports the implementation of the Practicum at the HRC, organizing the recruitment and on-boarding of students and the logistics of their immersive experience, and contributes to the teaching of the undergraduate student cohort.

In the international experience of Malawi, the emphasis on learning *through* human rights centers on student agency and autonomy in the research learning process. The Practicum provides students with knowledge and information prior to departure about rights-based approaches and sustainable development in Malawi. Once there, it requires undergraduate students to live in the local community and grapple with behavioral expectations and patterns while working in an intercultural team environment. They navigate a relationship with their Malawian teammates to create a shared process for interviewing local community members, such as Village Chiefs, local fisherman, vulnerable youth, women in markets, using language translation and non-verbal communication skills across cultural and gendered divides.

Students journal throughout the summer experience to promote reflection and develop strong bonds within the cohort. Many find it challenging to fully grapple with the realities of global economic inequality, the effects of colonization, the role of white westerners in African countries like Malawi, the failures of development aid and programming, as well as their personal identities and positions in taking the Practicum. Students who are majoring in non-social or humanities disciplines often acquire new confidence in their capacities to undertake research and advocacy. Some students report a complete transformation in their political or personal worldviews, shifting from conservative and narrow perspectives to openly progressive views or identities upon returning to campus.

With their data collected in Malawi, students return to campus to integrate their observations, experience, and information into a full research paper that analyzes the data and produces findings and recommendations. In this process, students need to evaluate the context of the NGO's program and determine how to best offer findings that are impactful. While some of the research produced does not directly change D2D programmatic decision-making, much of it has paved the way for specific and demonstrable changes in programs, program evaluation, or decisions to develop new programs.

In learning *for* human rights, graduate students make informed, ethical judgments about how to represent and frame issues facing Malawian youth in development to an external, primarily Western audience. They gain insight into development programming and the mechanics of funding and managing a local NGO in a developing context, by creating blog posts, social media content, newsletters to donors, and drafting grant proposals and annual reports. Each of these assignments requires the formulation of strong written communications skills using different styles, tone, and content. The yearlong presence in Malawi means cultivating relationships within the local community through collaboration and programming. This emerges as one of the most critically transformative dimensions of the experience.

ABOLITION OHIO

Locally, in the Miami Valley of southwestern Ohio, the HRC also provides the platform for a coalition on anti-trafficking known as Abolition Ohio (AO). AO works in partnership with concerned community members, law enforcement and service organizations in the Miami Valley and across the state and the country to prevent human trafficking, protect victims and survivors, and help prosecute the criminals responsible.

The work of AO consists of organizing coalition meetings that seek to coordinate various service providers in victim services, and also to ensure collaboration and awareness-raising with interested community members. AO contributes to state-level policy-making and legislative drafting forums through Commissions, conferences, and other convenings, providing expert inputs and advice. To establish an evidence base for its expert advice, AO conducts applied research projects aimed at improving the response to human trafficking.

AO also contributes to awareness-raising and teaching in the field of anti-trafficking in multiple ways. In the time of Covid-19, AO evolved its forums to include a dialogue on trafficking entitled, *Traffic Talk*, which provides a safe and supportive space for a wide range of people to discuss sensitive and advanced topics about human trafficking. Sessions consist of brief expert presentations, written, video and audio resources, and dialogue that emphasizes listening and understanding. It hosts a speakers bureau of trained and certified volunteers who give 'human trafficking 101' presentations to diverse audiences consisting of civic and nonprofit organizations, faith-based groups, businesses, and schools in the community. In addition, AO supports local schools and youth programs in the Miami Valley with the School Trafficking Outreach Program (STOP). STOP is aimed at preventing human trafficking in the Dayton area through awareness and education. The program educates, equips, and empowers youth, school personnel, and community members through interactive, engaging, and comprehensive anti-human trafficking program materials.

Students are engaged in the work of AO in multiple ways. A fully funded Graduate Assistantship is offered at the HRC for a student to work on AO covering all dimensions of the coalition's initiatives. Undergraduate students, often those who have been involved in an Anti-Trafficking course, are taken on by the HRC to work for AO. There are also ad hoc opportunities for student engagement, for example, students in the School of Education are trained to be STOP volunteers who go into middle and high schools to deliver anti-trafficking training materials.

Rooted in the local Dayton community, AO provides students with a broad experience across a range of advocacy spheres, with an emphasis on connecting and campaigning. Students undertake discrete tasks such as organizing and managing meetings, developing agendas, taking notes, and coordinating communication with community members, law enforcement and partner organizations. They also generate programmatic and educational content for social media platforms, and engage with other organizations with similar missions by intentionally liking, commenting on, and sharing content.

Students are required to develop skills in public presentation, awareness-raising and training, particularly adapting anti-trafficking training presentations for various audiences and updating materials with new and relevant content. As a campaign-based coalition, these trainings provide audiences with concrete action steps they can take to help prevent and respond to human trafficking. Students are also engaged in presenting at thematic conferences, writing blogs, and reflecting on what they have learned from these forums. The types of audiences students learn to present to are diverse, including civic engagement organizations, social service organizations, law enforcement, and near peer to peer middle, high school, and college students.

Students develop the capacity to engage with community volunteers in research for institutionalizing anti-trafficking policy and laws. For example, students have collaborated on an analysis of online commercial sex advertisements alongside legal researchers from Lexis-Nexis who volunteered to participate in the project. Students have also conducted an analysis of local commercial sex ads and life history interviews of local sex workers for a human trafficking prevalence report. Projects have also included research on youth prevention education and illicit massage businesses which have been used to influence and pressure policy-makers to take action.

As a community-based coalition, AO thrives on cultivating local ties and relationships with partner organizations and community members to raise awareness and stimulate preventative and responsive action. As essential to both learning *through* and *for* human rights, students gain the ability to reach across differences to bring diverse stakeholders together around shared commitments and in communal forums. Developing the capacities to design and facilitate community dialogues around sensitive issues like sexual exploitation are viewed by students as transformational. It has been deeply empowering for students to gain knowledge of the human rights violations involved in human trafficking along with the experience of how to seek to prevent and redress them.

Main Takeaways

While the potential for transformational learning is substantial from these high-impact programs, the challenges involved in providing this level of EL in academic settings are not inconsequential. From my perspective as Executive Director of the HRC, there are a number of lessons learned and practical issues which should be taken into account when designing and implementing experiential learning for HRE.

First, as a general point, it is important not to underestimate the human resource and financial costs involved in administering such intensive programs. Financial costs vary widely from domestic and international travel and accommodation, logistics, supporting partner organizations' contributions to the programs, materials, storage, and other production costs. Scholarships and remuneration are high costly items. These programs demand substantial logistical and administration support for effectively implementation.

Second and relatedly, high-quality faculty and staff engagement, mentoring, and support for students are essential to the transformative experience of these programs. This involves human resource costs, as well as time and opportunity costs. University settings will vary in terms of the capacities of Centers to engage and secure high-quality human rights knowledgeable faculty for teaching, mentoring, and ideation. The contours of the academic environment, the additional time that faculty have to allocate to these programs and whether this is incentivized through promotion and tenure, and clear affiliations are all elements that need to be taken into account, ideally during the initial design of programs.

Third, partnerships with international and domestic NGOs are at the heart of these programs, and effective and reciprocal partnerships require intense maintenance and care, in addition to implicating financial matters as mentioned above. This is time and resource intensive as well as relational work. Investment is required to ensure that the partnership is truly reciprocal, and not solely transactional on either side. The 'do no harm' principle which is foundational to human rights and humanitarian action is relevant for all these programs, and ethical considerations are implicated in all human rights advocacy work. Having a shared understanding of these dimensions is not always smooth across partnerships. However, working through them is critical for the programs to reach their aims in terms of human rights outcomes, as well as student experience. The book, *Community-Based Global Learning: The Theory and Practice of Ethical Engagement at Home and Abroad* (Hartman et al., 2018), provides essential conceptual and practical guidance in this field.

Fourth, these programs need to be tailored in part to the specific students who are the intended beneficiaries. A primary question to answer in the design phase is whether these students are from shared academic majors or experiences. In the case of the HRC, the programs are intended to provide EL in human rights education to a broad and diverse range of students from majors and minors across the University. While this can bring an additional layer of impact for students and faculty alike in experiencing truly interdisciplinary learning, the capacities within academia to provide high-quality and deeply interdisciplinary experiences vary widely. At the same time, it is important to ensure that the programs are grounded in appropriate levels of knowledge *about* human rights to be successful.

Fifth, these experiences can have profound impacts on students in terms of their recognition of their own power and privilege. Human rights advocacy is a field rife with mental health challenges, which include the nature and personal experiences of the individuals who are attracted to the work, the impact of secondary trauma on advocates, and the failures of the culture of advocacy to recognize these impacts and prioritize mental health for advocates (Mental Health Functioning in the Human Rights Field: Findings from an International Internet-Based Survey, Joscelyne et al., 2015). Lessons learned from the HRC program indicate that this process can be difficult and fraught for many students. Intentional ways to plan and address this in EL for HRE could include integrating robust reflection methods to be undertaken both individually and in cohorts, integrating evidence-based knowledge and scholarship about vicarious impact of trauma in human rights work into the program, and ensuring that self-care and mental health issues are tackled directly in the implementation of the experience.

Finally, one of the most challenging aspects of these programs comes in the assessment of program impact overall and specifically the evaluation of transformational learning outcomes. Quality assessment processes are essential to improving student experience and program evolution, and to measuring the impact of the programs in relation to human rights advocacy. One of the complexities is the need for assessment of impact and evaluation on multiple levels. These are (a) the individual student transformation at the time and at certain stages in the future, (b) the degree of transformational impact on the partners and the specific communities involved in the program, and (c) the effect on human rights advocacy or outcomes. Each of these levels requires appropriate and tailored tools and resources to implement them, including data analysis, and then the integration of the evaluation results back into the evolution of the program and the partnership.

CONCLUSION

The conception of HRE at the international level is comprehensive and transformative. Providing human rights education to youth is the goal of the World Program and SDG 4 on global citizenship education. To attain these far-reaching aims, EL must be integral to education on human rights at the tertiary level. For the HRC at the University of Dayton, HRE involves learning *about*, *through*, and *for* human rights advocacy. A number of high impact programs have been developed over time which seek to provide young people with the knowledge, skills, attitudes, values, perspectives, and behaviors that constitute human rights in practice. Lessons learned from those programs indicate they are challenging and resource intensive to design and implement successfully, but can be transformational for students, partners, and community advocates. Through these programs the HRC contributes to progress in reaching these global agendas. Despite these successes, the field of HRE in higher education remains nascent as it relates to EL. Based on HRC program experiences, I believe there is a world of potential and need for expansion and deepening of EL programming in HRE to fully realize the transformational promise of global agendas.

References

Banki, S., Valiente-Riedl, E., & Duffill, P. (2014). Teaching human rights at the tertiary level: Addressing the 'knowing–doing gap' through a role-based simulation approach. *Journal of Human Rights Practice, 6*(2), 387.

Budabin, A. C., & Pruce, J. R. (2018). The elite politics of media advocacy in human rights. *New Political Science, 40*(4), 744–762.

Florea-Hudson, N., & Pruce, J. R. (2020). We are all students: The moral courage project as a model for transdisciplinary experiential learning. In K. Lovett's (Ed.), *Diverse pedagogical approaches to experiential learning* (pp. 111–128). Palgrave Macmillan.

Flowers, N. (2000). *The human rights education handbook: Effective practices for learning, action, and change.* Human Rights Resource Center.

Hartman, E., Kiely, R., Boettcher, C., & Friedrichs, J. (2018). *Community-based global learning: The theory and practice of ethical engagement at home and abroad.* Stylus Publishing.

Joscelyne, A., Knuckey, S., Satterthwaite, M. L., Bryant, R. A., Li, M., Meng, Q., & Brown, A. D. (2015). Mental health functioning in the human rights field: Findings from an international internet-based survey. *PLoS One, 10*(12), e0145188.

Kurasawa, F. (2007). *The work of global justice: Human rights as practices.* Cambridge University Press.

Pruce, J. R. (2019). *The mass appeal of human rights.* Palgrave Macmillan.

Sharp, D. N. (2018, August). Pragmatism and multidimensionality in human rights advocacy. *Human Rights Quarterly, 40*(3), 499–520.

Tibbitts, F. (2005). Transformative learning and human rights education: Taking a closer look. *Intercultural Education, 16*(2), 107–113.

UN Human Rights Council. (2011). *United Nations declaration on human rights education and training: Resolution/adopted by the human rights council,* A/HRC/RES/16/1, Retrieved from https://documents-dds-ny.un.org/doc/UNDOC/GEN/N11/467/04/PDF/N1146704.pdf?OpenElement. [Accessed March 31, 2021].

Wurdinger, S. D., & Carlson, J. A. (2010). *Teaching for experiential learning: Five approaches that work.* Rowman & Littlefield Publishers.

Fostering Entrepreneurship, Creativity, and Problem-Solving Skills

CHAPTER 5

Alumni Engagement Through Applied Creativity: A Case Study

Brian LaDuca and Adrienne Ausdenmoore

This chapter is a reflective case study that demonstrates the practice of experiential learning (EL) partnership between University alumni and undergraduate students studying the applied creative skills that the most in-demand careers are seeking. Eyler (2009) explains how "experiential education blurs the line between theory and practice" (para. 19); this case study provides a working framework for students to practice creative skills in an alumni program that could lure graduates, regardless of era, to connect across disciplinary silos and engage directly with students from design to evolution to positive return on partnership. I am Brian LaDuca, Executive Director of the Institute of Applied Creativity for Transformation (IACT) and administrative faculty at the University of Dayton (UD). Together with my colleague and co-author of this chapter, Adrienne Ausdenmoore, Director of IACT, we are driven to prepare students across any discipline of study for today's ever-changing workforce.

B. LaDuca • A. Ausdenmoore (✉)
Institute of Applied Creativity for Transformation, University of Dayton, Dayton, OH, USA
e-mail: bladuca1@udayton.edu; aausdenmoore1@udayton.edu

© The Author(s), under exclusive license to Springer Nature Switzerland AG 2022
K. Lovett (ed.), *Diverse Pedagogical Approaches to Experiential Learning, Volume II*,
https://doi.org/10.1007/978-3-030-83688-7_5

Introduction to IACT

The Institute of Applied Creativity for Transformation (IACT) is an academic institute at UD that trains students in the creative competencies of critical thinking, complex problem-solving, and cross-disciplinary collaboration—while applying those same skills to the students' diverse disciplines of study. As the founding leadership team of the Institute, we piloted our applied creativity curriculum in 2014, a process that included nearly 60 faculty, staff, and Dayton community partners in its development.

In 2016, the World Economic Forum indicated that the three skills that would be in the highest demand by 2020 were complex problem-solving, critical thinking, and creativity. These skills not only teach students how to confront problems in an ever-complex world, but more importantly help students understand how to think, which is imperative to all types of EL opportunities (Kolb, 1984). Yet the skills identified globally as most important to creative problem-solving are currently playing a minimal role in most curricula (Adobe, 2018). Through an adaptive framework that centers on building these creative competencies, we developed a transcripted academic certificate in applied creativity, the first of its kind in higher education. The certificate is open to undergraduate students of all majors, and graduated its first class of students in May 2018. As of May 2020, 35 students have successfully completed the certificate, with an additional 67 currently enrolled.

The Institute's applied creativity pedagogy, while uniquely designed within the UD, has its roots in principles of design thinking—a methodology that originated at Stanford University's d.school. Design thinking is an approach to innovation that stems from an empathetic "people first" (p. 87) mindset and early prototyping/testing as the keys to learning and product development (Brown, 2008). The iterative process employed by the students at IACT approaches creative problem-solving through a cycle of active experimentation and reflective observation, as described in Kolb's (1984) EL cycle.

Students training with IACT continue to study in their disciplinary field while developing their own personal DRIVE: a map for vocational discernment of one's own meaning that can actionize a student's Passion, Purpose, and Possibility. Baxter Magolda's (2001, 2009) research shows that self-authorship benefits all learners because they are able to manage the dynamic complexities of their academic knowledge and their experiential engagement. The mentoring and advising model developed at IACT embraces the recursive and iterative dialog between students and educators around skills, talents, passions, and visions. The DRIVE engages students by navigating their relational knowledge, human engagement, and critical reflection of self, based off of UD's holistic educational philosophy and Singleton's (2015) Head, Heart, and Hands Model for Transformational Learning. The DRIVE is vocationally centered with a long-term relational process that guides one's focus away from "what" you are going to do with your life but rather on the sense of being, or "who" you are working toward.

The integrated curriculum of the IACT certificate emphasizes the whole of a student's experience, rather than simply the context of their chosen major or a specific course subject. As a result, even simple class exercises provide the potential for immediate and meaningful application. This "framing" (Roberts, 2016, pp. 92–94) brings the real world into the classroom while simultaneously engaging students in critical reflection about the experiences that they are partaking in. Still, students who self-select into the IACT program are diverse. Students seeking a sense of belonging, students who identify as "go-getters," and students who are looking for that career advantage are all part of the program. For many of them the focus is on the creative skills, and for others it's the ability to be vulnerable with intention; in all cases, the student-centered approach to their lived and learned experiences is key.

The 13-credit hour certificate culminates in a two-part EL cornerstone, known as ACT III: Vocational Innovation and ACT IV: Innovative Transformation. The course focuses on the practice of key competencies and development of creative solutions that apply students' DRIVEs to societal issues and challenges. The students come from a wide variety of majors and learn to work effectively with peers from other disciplines to develop a shared learning experience. This transdisciplinary approach "dissolves the boundaries between the conventional disciplines and organizes teaching and learning around the construction of meaning in the context of real-world problems or themes" (UNESCO International Bureau of Education, 2013, p. 58).

Problem-solving skills and the ability to work on a team have been identified as key resume attributes for employers (NACE, 2020). The introduction of an Alumni Influencer program, launched in fall of 2019, provides alumni and other interested champions of our work an opportunity to 'give back' as a mentor by contributing to the growth and sustainability of the student experience and the entire academic institute (Wenger,

1998). The program engages alumni to guide a student team toward successful completion of their transdisciplinary cornerstone projects during the final year in the certificate program. Through this one-year commitment, the influencers connect their own background, current work, and lived experience with the students' DRIVEs.

The process for the inaugural Alumni Influencer program was an ongoing experience that saw many iterations in its first year. As executive director, I have observed that even in its early stages, the Alumni Influencer program has provided our students a tremendous value-add in gaining real-world insights and experiences that connect to their own vocation and self-authorship while connecting with an alumnus on a deeper level. As emerging research continues to detail the importance of creative skill acquisition and application within the workforce, it is as important that students in our program also have a deep understanding of themselves. This act of vulnerability is a key component for developing a true trust for idea development, and the attempts to teach this early in the program have proven positively evident in our upperclassmen when they enter our Alumni Influencer program.

LAYING THE GROUNDWORK FOR ALUMNI ENGAGEMENT

In the Fall of 2018, shortly after IACT's first nine undergraduates completed the certificate, many units across the University began to grow curious about the impact and outcomes of such a novel and new academic institute. One specific area that was especially focused on the IACT was University Advancement, which includes Alumni Relations. The interdisciplinarity of our institute provided a much larger landscape for alumni interest and involvement, and a mutual interest between IACT and Advancement to engage UD alumni of any generation was a very strong catalyst for further investigation.

Traditionally, Advancement/Alumni Relations will begin relationship building with the intention to procure donations in the form of gifts and scholarships. Instead, our Alumni Influencer program stemmed from alumni who were interested in the learning, the innovative approach to teaching, and the student growth and application. They were excited about the cross-disciplinary structure of engineers working with education majors, and philosophy majors working with exercise science majors. For me, I did not want to build new relationships simply to fund another program. What I wanted was an alumni family that could give actual credence to the developing creative mindset of students from across all majors of the University. Money would be nice. A sustainable and evolving relationship would be preferred, for it models the importance of a transformative, people-to-people relationship that focuses on the applied creative competencies of resilience, empathy and initiative versus the more common transactional people-to-product relationship that tends to dominate most innovation and entrepreneurial programs.

A supportive colleague in Advancement took the initiative to begin an introductory process for alumni who shared in the IACT mindset and design thinking inspired approaches to complex problem-solving. She began to communicate with alumni within the entrepreneurial, education, creativity, and design sectors—focusing specifically on those "outside the box" thinkers and creators who would have thrived in IACT if it had existed during their time as undergraduate students. This approach might seem vast, expansive, and ambiguous—and it was. Still, we began to find those alumni who thrived in such creative and ambiguous spaces and who understood the purpose and intended impact on the next generation of UD alumni. One such alumnus, an aspirational human whose life at that point had taken him across the business sectors into health, was the type of creative thinker that we hope the next generation of students will become. Our initial conversation provided the scaffolding for what is known today as the IACT Alumni Influencer program. By the end of that summer, we had six Influencers ready to pilot the first program.

CONNECTING STUDENTS WITH ALUMNI

A formalized "Roundtable" experience was scheduled for November 2019, where the 6 Influencers came from across the country to the UD campus to meet with the 14 IACT certificate students during their regularly scheduled ACT III course. The students sat in a circle, interspersed with our Influencers and the IACT staff. It was an informally designed affair situated in the IACT's own Creator Space, a flexible space for quick and dirty iterative practices of creative innovation, with walls covered in glass boards for sketching and note-taking and a color scheme more akin to a children's museum than a college classroom.

A video camera was placed in the room to assure an archive of the dialog at the Roundtable would be captured for never before had we led such a public forum on vulnerability and the application of it through creative skills. The students were prompted to provide a story that connected their meaning-making practices within the DRIVE and their academic process and aspirations. The practice of storytelling was not new to any of the students in the room for each, by this time, had spent between nine to twelve hours of individual discernment with me. The action of storytelling with a larger group of colleagues and strangers was new. Yet each student reached deep into their passions, purposes, and possibilities and shared for five to ten minutes on what drives them to be who they are. For example, one student shared that her DRIVE was to:

> impact long term health outcomes for patients experiencing chronic pain through preventative care. As a student in the Pre-Medicine Program at UD, I was surrounded by incredibly driven and focused students whose goal was to get into medical school, physician's assistant school, pharmacy school, etc. While I admired the work ethic of my peers, I felt disconnected from them in that I knew my passion for engaging in healthcare went beyond simply becoming a physician or physician's assistant... I took health policy courses, social work courses, health communication courses, anything to help to understand the unique challenges that patients and healthcare providers face today. I enjoyed all of these courses, and learned a lot from them, but none of them gave me the space to imagine, dream, create, or innovate a future.

The authenticity in the room was felt by the Influencers who worked to ask follow-up questions that were not aimed as critiques of the story but more open-ended inquiries that pushed the students to seek a bit more tangible connection to the Influencers own work experience. Three hours of engagement between current students and alumni brought out deep levels of motivation, discipline, and ambiguity. The emotions were very high due to the tremendous amount of respect given by each and every human in the Creator Space that late November afternoon. More importantly, connections between students and alumni were unearthed. This was the start of the transformative, person-to-person relationship I sought to develop between alumni and our academic program. Money, investment, or scholarships were never addressed but rather obstacles, dreams, and aspirations were partnered in ways that a traditional student/alumni relationship may not find time to develop.

The outcome of this Roundtable was to create small cohorts of students whose stories found authentic connection with alumni Influencers in attendance. The process was quite organic and lacked pretension. I simply asked each Influencer if there was a single student who they felt most connected to from the Roundtable. This provided all Influencers an opportunity to review their hopes for specific student pairings and trios that they, as experienced professionals in various fields, could leverage to make possible innovative change in their own work and fields. Each Influencer was ultimately matched with a group of two or three diverse students.

One cohort example consisted of a senior pre-med major whose story revolved around women's reproductive rights, a senior finance major invested in blockchain technology for more inclusive economic exchange and a senior human resources major who, due to financial pressures, had to leave campus early and whose story was still in great transition. Their influencer was the previously mentioned alumnus who was in the innovative health industry out of Boston. The transactional outcome from this cohort was not supposed to be determined at this time but the transformative relationship was just starting. The new student cohorts would spend the remainder of the semester connecting their DRIVEs and disciplinary work together with their Influencer, in order to develop a clear collaborative project idea that would address real-world problems or themes. One student shared the following about the relationship with his Influencer:

> Early on in our work together, it became apparent that I was seen as a part of their team and they valued my unique perspective. It takes humility to admit that you do not have all the answers and seek outside help. I was able to ideate, brainstorm, rough draft, prototype, and present my ideas pertinent to employing people overcoming traumatic life events... This challenge forced me to do a lot of internal reflection and come from a position of both understanding and empathy.

THE AMBIGUITY OF A NEW PROCESS

Our first hiccup in this new program would begin to emerge at this point. As the fall semester neared an end, it was apparent that the next steps for Influencer engagement with the students were quite unclear. The students were both distracted with end of the semester demands and my unclear direction. Their communication back to their respective Influencers was minimal. The Influencers began asking questions around who should guide the relational process, the students or the Influencer. Some Influencers just jumped in and took the lead; others were less ambitious, afraid to interfere with overall program goals. My comfort with ambiguity translated as unclear, and because of that the act of developing a true understanding of the Influencers, their students, and the specific real-world challenge they were to work on was not 100% successful by the time the students left for winter break.

At the start of 2020, it was imperative that the Influencer group had a balance of understanding and empowerment when working directly with their respective student teams. Due to the lack of what Kolb (1984) calls "abstract conceptualism," any final stage of understanding the relationships between the student, the Influencer, and how they were going to create a transferability for their own practices was going to be nearly impossible because of this unclear start. An IACT Influencer Starter Pack was created to bridge that gap which provided the vocabulary, the mission, visions, pedagogy, and creative exercises that the students would begin working on in the spring semester—with the goal for the Starter Pack to aid in explaining those IACT specific models to help develop a shared understanding of what was a very emerging program.

The weekly work between the Influencers and their respective student teams would cover the following over the course of the spring semester:

- **Challenge Statement:** Working from the Roundtable and the collaboration between students' DRIVEs and their Influencer's experience, a "How Will We" statement was created to understand the initial plan and outcome.
- **DRIVE Collision:** Each student team identified the intersections between each other's DRIVE statements and how those intersections provide a shared vocational goal among the students.
- **First Lens Solution:** Students developed an initial idea for deliverable that should seek to solve the challenge, give disciplinary direction, and satisfy the Influencer's overall goal.
- **Necessities:** Students were asked to develop a simple story wherein their discipline and DRIVE were put into a realistic position to satisfy both the challenge and the first lens solution. Common unknowns and tensions that were shared between the student teams were then recognized as necessary to the continued research and development.
- **DRIVE Actions:** Students revisited their own vocational mapping to determine how their Purpose + Passion, Passion + Possibility, and Possibility + Purpose could be leveraged to help address the necessities.

- **Leverage Points:** The student's common DRIVE actions and their addressing of the necessities were then transformed into very specific themes and concepts that would become the tangible frameworks for the next iteration of the Challenge Solution.
- **Field Tests:** Working specifically with their Influencer's network of contacts and potential recipients of the final deliverable, students would build on-the-ground experiences to test the leverage points identified to assure these are the key needs being addressed within the challenge and solution.

The weekly experiential collaboration between the Influencers and the students found a great rhythm between January through early March. Concepts, ideas, and even field tests were being scheduled in order to leave a solid month to assess the field test results with Influencers and finish designing and building the needed solution. On Thursday March 12, UD declared a pause on face-to-face teaching due to the emerging COVID-19 pandemic. Immediately, we were faced with moving to a virtual format and developing a plan for doing so successfully. Cohort groups had already scheduled field tests that now had to be canceled. One group was exploring ways to cater to different student learning styles, and had planned to interview and prototype tests for grade school educators in Indianapolis. Another team conducting a large-scale survey around college accessibility had planned to follow up in person; this now had to move to a virtual format that no one was prepared for. More importantly, the one-on-one weekly meetings between the cohorts and I were now going to be fully virtual—but when to reschedule and how much time would be left in the semester to do so was left without answer.

THE PIVOT TO ONLINE

Eleven days after the University's COVID-19 announcement and a scheduled spring break, communication with the certificate students resumed. While much interaction with the Influencers had already been in a virtual format, we understood that navigating this new normal of online coursework was a load the students were not expecting. The goal was to balance both the deflating sense of student morale with a creative, innovative, and transferable method for certificate completion.

I communicated with all Influencers to lay out a prospective plan for the next steps that specifically asked how we could assure that their wants, needs, and visions were still supported. We set up a series of Zoom calls to assure communication and support were both clean and inspired for all invested in the program. This would give the students as well as the Influencers, who too were going through transitions of their own due to the pandemic, the time to get other needed priorities in order before returning to the creative and innovative work they had developed earlier in the year.

From the moment the pandemic disrupted the program, we were prepared for the student teams and their Influencers to create, design, and deliver on the work in whatever new state they still found passion and purpose in. The active experimentation during these final weeks of work took on a much broader sense of transferability. The one-on-one weekly meetings with me pivoted to weekly Zoom calls for each Influencer and their students. I began joining the calls to observe and get a sense of commitment while also seeing how much, if any, of the work done during class pre-COVID was still valuable and relevant. To my surprise, the work found continued momentum and even more importantly, purpose and value for the students and their Influencers. As one student shared,

> I have learned that we cannot continue to keep approaching the same challenges from the same perspective, but maybe from a different angle. We need to change the way we even approach the problems, and that is what my group challenged me to consider. Our team relationship with our influencer was honestly stronger and more influential than I anticipated it to be.

The purposeful learning that was occurring at this point has always been the intent of the IACT, but we understood that getting the collaborative work between students and their Influencer completed was going to be top priority during the pandemic. Yet, as we pleasantly discovered, the usefulness and relevance of the learning was less about the product deliverable for the Influencer but the strengthening of relationship, practicing incorporating diverse perspectives and the exhibiting of flexibility became the learning most useful to students' life (Kolb, 1984). The Influencers also highlighted the importance of students practicing skills and developing professional experience:

> [Bringing together] the diversity of thoughts and opinions, interests and passions ... is much more realistic to what happens out in the professional world than you get in a traditional higher education academic setting.

One of the benefits of a program like IACT is that it brings to the forefront that solving problems is not a straight line… These students will be set up with a skill set that is needed in the workplace: understanding themselves… [and] understanding how to solve problems holistically from a place of empathy.

Each student team and Influencer met at a minimum of five times over Zoom, where they continued to build tangible results around their earlier semester work. The canceled field tests were still designed but not necessarily executed face to face due to pandemic restrictions. Collaborative concepts went through a true iterative process and then developed. Design companies were brought into work closely on storyboards, and one cohort even pitched their medical application to a set of medical venture capitalists in Boston to experience the action of sharing a medical/business technology concept and to get a sense of viability and feasibility. After this pitch, one student shared:

In reality, my team's final deliverable could never come to fruition without a massive shift in funding and ideologies in the U.S. healthcare system, but instead of encouraging us to maneuver within an already broken system, Addison (Influencer) encouraged us to be the change we want to see.

At the end of the semester, a virtual ceremony was held to debut the final deliverables for this graduating class. Here, each Influencer was able to introduce their students, their process and their deliverable. Each student team had to present their concepts and provide an appropriate human-centered story around their work, reinforcing the program's emphasis on the people-to-people relationships and personal development within their process. One Influencer team shared the following:

Once we got involved with IACT and the Influencer Program, we truly became enmeshed in the fabric of the University of Dayton and its mission of Learn, Lead, Serve. We value the real-world experience the University offers to the students and the challenge to think outside of academia into the future, taking into consideration the real humans they'll be working with as they grow into professionals.

This two-hour event was a perfect punctuation of a very odd and challenging semester that saw students working experientially in a direct and hands-on fashion, only to pivot into a virtual EL model that no one had ever experienced prior.

Lessons Learned and Moving Forward

This inaugural year of the program illustrated that there is great potential in how our certificate students can engage with alumni in meaningful ways that further their personal and professional developments. We also discovered that largely, the process and practice of the creative competencies our Institute was built on—critical thinking, complex problem-solving, and collaboration with others—was the primary measure of impact, rather than the project deliverables themselves. That said, three of the projects continued to be developed with Influencers in our summer micro-internship program, where the skill-building and networking continued with a different set of students.

We have learned that the ambiguity that we, as leaders of the Institute, thrive on, proved to be challenging for Influencers. This was compounded by overly complex vocabulary that participants struggled to keep up with. As we move into our second year of the Influencer program, we have spent considerable time honing in on the key concepts that shape our curriculum and a simpler, more accessible vocabulary. This, combined with more clearly defined outcomes, should provide new Influencers a more direct path into our process and hopefully fewer challenges in the future. Reflecting on the relationships that were built, one student shared

> I continue to think about my work differently... I am starting to think about how corporations play a role for good in these societal challenges, which is new for me. This is why I reached out to our influencer after the program ended... They said they would always be willing to talk and impart whatever advice and wisdom they may have to me. I think our influencer sees the opportunities we have as students, how we think, and what we want to do with our lives, and they want to support that growth so that we can truly make a difference in the world.

For the Influencers, one identified benefit was that the program offered an opportunity for them to reconnect with their alma mater. Several cited a direct connection to the University and its students that they had not experienced previously:

IACT has given me an exciting opportunity to reconnect with the University of Dayton in ways I have previously not been able to... I found the energy, vision and purpose of the students to be really fulfilling and exciting to be around.

IACT has been such a great way to connect back to the University in a way that I haven't been able to do in previous years. [It] created an opportunity to engage myself in a program that I wish existed when I was a student.

Despite the challenging circumstances of the spring semester, the program also demonstrated the potential for alumni impact through virtual engagement. This discovery has led to an ongoing series of "Influencer Lunch Lounges" where we invite alumni and other Institute supporters to engage with our certificate students in a casual networking discussion via Zoom. This is one of several tactics that have helped shape a new alumni engagement strategy for our Institute. We still face the challenge of scalability and sustaining momentum with alumni participation, especially as our certificate student population grows. However, we feel confident that new strategies will build a larger pool of interested alumni that then funnels deeper engagement and advocacy for our Institute. The response we received from Influencers regarding their relationship with the University mirrors the outcomes in other student-alumni mentorship programs, providing a path for strategic alumni engagement that leads to long-term support (Vieregger and Bryant, 2020).

As other institutions continue to expand what alumni relations can mean for experiential learning, the Influencer Program developed at our university is a model that can provide various new points of entry. As highlighted throughout the chapter, this program was not developed to raise money, but rather, to raise awareness and build relationships. There is no denying the importance of continued fundraising and financial gifts from interested alumni and champions of the University but the Influencer Program put greater emphasis on the alumni/student partnership. This approach empowered new alumni who perhaps were not in a position to give financially to still contribute time and experience, from which the students were able to learn and practice from. Engaging young alumni can be challenging; this program not only connects alumni to students, but also builds around the alumni skillset—giving value to what they can contribute versus what they feel they should contribute (which is usually financial).

For the students, the opportunity to work in a digital experiential format with alumni shifted perspectives as to what a meaningful alumni/student experience can be. The pivot to online shed new light on the power of digital formats as a way to create a consistent line of communication even when alumni partners are geographically distanced from the University. The practice of online EL does have its limitations, but the accessibility of such alumni should be recognized as a potential new way to spark and maintain meaningful student engagement. It is not necessary to have a robust travel budget in order to connect students to alumni over geographical boundaries. This program has spun off other virtual engagements such as lunch and learns and Friday Happy Hour dialogues that have brought together dozens of alumni on a consistent basis who would have never found the time or the money to do so in person. Today, our students know they can reach out and talk to alumni and other institutional champions from Seattle to Orlando if and when their learning needs it. In closing, we feel that we have developed a framework for our Institute and other universities across the nation that advances the experiential learning impact on our students as well as providing meaningful engagement for alumni.

REFERENCES

Adobe. (2018). *Creative problem solving in schools* [Global study]. http://cps.adobeeducate.com/GlobalStudy

Baxter Magolda, B. M. (2001). *Making their own way: Narratives for transforming higher education to promote self-development.* Stylus.

Baxter Magolda, B. M. (2009). *Authoring your life: Developing an internal voice to navigate life's challenges.* Stylus.

Brown, T. (2008). Design thinking. *Harvard Business Review, 86*(6), 84–92.

Eyler, J. (2009). The power of experiential education. *Liberal Education, 95*(4). https://www.aacu.org/publications-research/periodicals/power-experiential-education

Kolb, D. A. (1984). *Experiential learning: Experience as the source of learning and development.* Prentice Hall.

NACE staff. (2020). *Key attributes employers want to see on students' resumes.* National Association of Colleges and Employers. https://www.naceweb.org/talent-acquisition/candidate-selection/key-attributes-employers-want-to-see-on-students-resumes/

Roberts, J. W. (2016). *Experiential education in the college context: What it is, how it works, and why it matters.* Routledge.

Singleton, J. (2015). Head, heart and hands model for transformative learning: Place as context for changing sustainability values. *Journal of Sustainability Education*, 1. http://www.susted.com/wordpress/content/head-heart-and-hands-model-for-transformative-learning-place-as-context-for-changing-sustainability-values_2015_03/

UNESCO International Bureau of Education. (2013). Transdisciplinary approach. In *IBE glossary of curriculum terminology*. http://www.ibe.unesco.org/en/glossary-curriculum-terminology/

Vieregger, C., & Bryant, A. (2020). Student-alumni mentoring in the business capstone: An opportunity to both cap and bridge the undergraduate experience. *Journal of Education for Business, 95*(5), 335–343. https://doi.org/10.1080/08832323.2019.1646700

Wenger, E. (1998). *Communities of practice: Learning, meaning, and identity.* Cambridge University Press.

World Economic Forum (2016). *The future of jobs: Employment skills and workforce strategy for the fourth industrial revolution* [Report]. http://www3.weforum.org/docs/WEF_Future_of_Jobs.pdf

An Experiential Learning Revolution: Engaging Business Students with Diverse Digital and Non-Digital Immersive Experiences with Not-for-Profit and for-Profit Organizations

Irene J. Dickey

Though I very much like to develop and deliver lectures, experiential learning (EL) has a vital role in University of Dayton's (UD) School of Business Administration (SBA) curriculum. EL is documented as part of our core values and strategic goals and objectives. The SBA's commitment to EL is stated in the following:

> Experiential Learning: The Key to Practical Wisdom. You wouldn't expect someone to become a top chef just by reading recipes from a cookbook, or a fighter pilot to know how to fly an F-16 by watching videos of other pilots. In the same way, we don't expect our students to learn business acumen

I. J. Dickey (✉)
Management & Marketing, University of Dayton, Dayton, OH, USA
e-mail: idickey1@udayton.edu

© The Author(s), under exclusive license to Springer Nature
Switzerland AG 2022
K. Lovett (ed.), *Diverse Pedagogical Approaches to Experiential
Learning, Volume II*,
https://doi.org/10.1007/978-3-030-83688-7_6

from a textbook – we expect them to learn by doing. Providing meaningful opportunities for all our students to engage in experiential learning is a key part of our Mission and Featured Programs and Initiatives at the University of Dayton. (University of Dayton, 2021, Experiential Learning section)

While it is evident that EL is valued at UD and the SBA, it is important to consider why EL is valuable for students. Before coming to UD, students and their anxious parents are presented with the concept that EL will be part of their educational experience. At the same time, it is clear that they may not understand what EL is and how it can benefit students. This chapter will provide an overview of the various EL strategies I use in my courses, including simulations and client projects, and some of the ways these EL experiences have benefitted student learning.

EL FOR DIVERSE LEARNING STYLES

Early on in my teaching career, I was influenced by the work of David Kolb who wrote about learning from experience. Kolb and Kolb (2005) define EL as "the process whereby knowledge is created through the transformation of experience. Knowledge results from the combinations of grasping and transforming the experience." Kolb and other scholars who preceded him (including Dewey, Lewin, and Piaget) placed experience at the center of the learning process. Kolb and Kolb (2011) envisioned a learner-centered educational system "based on a learning cycle driven by the resolution of the dual dialectics of action/reflection and experience/abstraction." This holistic theory defines learning as the major process of human adaptation involving the whole person (Kolb & Kolb, 2012).

In his EL model, Kolb describes two different ways of *grasping* experience: abstract conceptualization and concrete experience. He also identifies two ways of *transforming* experience: active experimentation and reflective observation. These four modes of learning are often portrayed as a cycle in which concrete experience provides information that serves as a basis for reflection; from these reflections, we assimilate information and form abstract concepts. People then use these concepts to develop new theories about the world, which they then actively test (Kolb, 1984).

As I reflected upon Kolb's models and how to implement EL in my courses, new digital EL opportunities were also beginning to emerge. When considering how to do EL effectively, it is important to take into consideration the dynamic nature of society, technology, and more. In thinking about the ever-changing landscape of the marketing and business world, I have found that it is important to continuously assess the effectiveness of different EL approaches over time. It became clear after trying different EL activities that preferred learning styles differ among students and that I needed to accommodate preferences with a range of EL models as much as possible. That is what I set out to do.

First, I wanted to gain a better understanding of these variations in students' learning styles and preferences. When considering Kolb's four learning styles: Diverger, Assimilator, Converger, and Accommodator, I tried to become more aware of the strengths and weaknesses of each when creating instructional materials and methods and what motivates students. Students within the learning style of The Accommodator are do-ers and enjoy putting plans into action immediately and seeing real-time results. Opposite of the Accommodator, the Assimilators possess the characteristics of working to gain understanding and to develop theoretical models/scenarios. Convergers are those you look toward to turn theories and ideas into reality as they are highly skilled in the practical application of ideas and tend to do best in situations with a problem that requires a singular, ideal solution.

And finally, Divergers. According to Tritsch (2020), students with this learning style excel at visualizing the "big picture" and organizing smaller bits of information into a meaningful whole. Kolb (1984) finds that learners generally prefer one of the styles above the others. Although Kolb thought of these learning styles as a continuum that one moves through over time, "usually people come to prefer, and rely on, one style above the others. Kolb's research finds that it is these main styles that instructors need to be aware of when creating instructional materials" (Concrete/Reflective/Abstract/Active – David Kolb, n.d.). Ultimately, one of the main benefits of EL is that it appeals to many different kinds of learning styles and preferences.

To be effective experiential educators, we must pay attention to what young people are actually doing and how they feel about what they are doing. EL is most effective when we can influence both feelings and emotions as well as students' knowledge and skills. Noticing and teasing out students' feelings and emotions and learning why students react the way they do, is an important part of being an experiential educator. By tuning into students' feelings and emotions, we can more effectively connect and guide students through EL, thereby deepening their learning. In the following sections, I discuss two primary EL experiences I regularly integrate in my courses: simulations and client projects. In my experience, these experiences effectively engage students' feelings and emotions and appeal to the various learning styles described above.

DISCOVERING SIMULATIONS AS AN EFFECTIVE EL APPROACH FOR BUSINESS STUDENTS

In my early years of teaching business courses, EL methods recommended by academic texts were limited to case studies and a few other assets. As I began to explore different ways of integrating EL in my courses, I turned to partnerships I had developed over the years with publishers, practitioners, and academics in the business field, who opened my eyes to various instructional material resources. Armed with this information and other academic resources on subjects such as the internet, social media, and gaming, I realized new opportunities for instruction and learning were emerging quickly. Today, textbook publishers and tech brands provide examples of simulations and games that are robust, relevant, and interesting.

Simulations involve students taking on new roles and models of behavior to gain a better understanding of that behavior (Baker et al., 2017). Through simulations in my business courses, students are assigned roles as buyers and sellers of some good or service. Students often use simulations to make predictions about the social, economic, or natural world. Because simulations increase student engagement and motivations, they may also "lead to deeper learning and greater long term retention of the class material" (Auman, 2011, p. 160). Simulations require students and instructors to communicate openly and frequently throughout the learning process; they involve "actively engaging in student-student or instructor-student conversations" and thus "by their very nature cannot be passive learning" (Why Teach with Simulations? 2020).

My first ah ha moment with simulations was hearing from students how a colleague of mine used The Lemonade Stand simulation game in class. In this online game, students decide how to price each cup of lemonade and how many pitchers to make. Students play (in teams or individually) through seven days and try to make as much profit as possible, subtracting the cost of the lemonade made from the income students earn from sales. There are three levels of difficulty: on easy, demand for lemonade is always high. At medium and hard, the weather changes to affect demand, and there are newspaper stories about world events that affect people's attitudes toward lemonade. The learning objective was to teach about money, budgeting, and profit. Simulations such as these are not only fun for most students but also effective in helping achieve business course learning outcomes. Through experiential simulations, students often achieve greater planning, presentation, teamwork, and analytical skills.

In my own courses, I use a social media management simulation, a search engine marketing (SEM) simulation, and a simulation for marketing a medical device. First, I guide students through the experience to help them get a better understanding of how these simulation platforms work. Students access simulations with a link provided by the publisher (such as Stukent or Harvard Business Publishing), and log on to their own account. They open up to a dashboard displaying the current status of the simulation and begin a new round of decision-making. During the simulation, students are active participants in selecting parameter values, anticipating outcomes, and formulating new questions to ask. Examples of parameter values include what is the budget; how much will I modify the product; and at what price shall I offer the product? The simulations allow students to observe various "what-if" scenarios by manipulating parameter values, after which they can anticipate outcomes. Additionally, simulations can provide students with the ability to transfer knowledge to new problems and situations. A well-done simulation is constructed to include an extension to a new problem or new set of parameters that requires students to extend what they have learned in an earlier context.

Through simulations, students also gain a greater understanding of their own thought processes. Simulations require students to think about how and why they behaved as they did during the simulation. As part of the simulation EL experience, students in my courses reflect on behaviors and actions in each simulation round. In the simulations I use, students play ten or more rounds of a business task such as managing the social media account of a fictitious retail company over the course of a semester. At first, they often seem quite lost and impatient; according to one of my students, "at first I had no idea what I was doing, but ultimately there was so much benefit…" Most students don't like reading or watching introductions and instructions and they want to get right to it. To be honest, most ignore these tools. Generally, I have found that the best form of introducing a simulation is for me to present a live demonstration to students. In some cases, I work alongside students and we manipulate their simulation together.

Setting simulations up as a competition worth significant course points increases their motivation and performance. Simulations also provide an abundance of data, which can be used to assess students learning. The analytics engines in these simulations record, analyze, and provide a detailed report on the participants' progress, results, and interaction throughout the simulation. In my assessment of student learning through simulations, I add a subjective evaluation based on each of the items in the report, and also take into account the conversations and communications students have shared with me about their simulation experience during the semester.

Student feedback on simulations in my courses has been overwhelmingly positive. Students have told me that when potential employers see EL simulations on their resumes, it becomes a major talking point and their interviewer often says "I wish they had this when I was in school!" Many clearly become involved and want to play more rounds of the simulation. Another benefit is that simulations are not as common as one might think, and students enjoy the diversity of course content and the novelty of the experience.

Without a doubt, integrating simulations of these strategies requires significant learning and preparation on my part in addition to regular course preparation. Nonetheless, I have found that EL goes beyond classroom learning and ensures that there is a high level of retention, thereby lifting a traditional learning program.

CLIENT PROJECTS AS AN EFFECTIVE EL OPPORTUNITY

In addition to simulations, I also invite guest speakers or "clients" to my courses to share their insights, experiences, and relevant case studies. Client projects which incorporate guest speakers, case studies, and group work have been shown to enhance student learning, and they also receive positive feedback from students (Rooks & Holliman, 2018). In my courses, students have the opportunity to work with local and national clients to help solve their marketing problems. While there are different models for conducting such projects, I incorporate both for-profit and not-for-profit clients and operate in the more traditional classroom setting where students are placed in teams and work over the semester to understand and solve a client business problem. My students have worked with organizations such as Proctor & Gamble (a world leader in consumer-packaged goods with brands such as Tide, Old Spice, and Crest), Nike, Totes, and United Way. Business-to-business clients (e.g., industrial products) are not as "sexy" as consumer brands. Nevertheless, many of my students will work in the business-to-business space and the learning which occurs while working with these clients is vital.

During the client projects, student teams are required to collaborate with their client, conduct substantive research, and deliver a professional caliber presentation. Students learn best practices for developing a business presentation that is professional rather than academic. For example, if teams are using a PowerPoint, they are taught not to read off their slides or include more than 30 words on a slide—visuals are more impactful than text. They learn to include an agenda and a conclusion in their presentations; I also teach them to welcome and thank the clients. These activities are designed to create student engagement by immersing them in a brand strategy-based problem-solving experience that requires collaboration with myself, the client, and student teams. Clients align their cases with topics such as product innovation, social media strategies, and how to rank on Google, for example, and they engage students in enthusiastic question and answer sessions.

Client projects are also opportunities for universities to create long-lasting, mutually beneficial relationships with businesses (Cooke & Williams, 2004). Client projects facilitate communication between academia and business, enlist the services of professionals in a variety of fields to help shape the education of future graduates, and offer opportunities for students to gain practical experience and keep instructors in touch with business trends and practices (Cooke & Williams, 2004). Employers see students' experience working with client projects as invaluable; many students have remarked that these client projects are what employers are most interested in learning more about during job interviews.

With regard to collaboration, I am currently working on a project with a client that requires students to meet with their client every two weeks. Evaluations are shared and will be used to help students develop the final project for presentation to the client. As I am writing this, I am wondering how presentations will be different using Zoom because of remote learning due to COVID-19. I expect them to be professional although one student recently presented with her team while in bed, and I think she was wearing pajamas. The upside is that clients can be located all over the world (and often have been). The in-person interaction side of working with others has always seemed to be most effective, however, we are learning how to optimize our communications. Just recently a client for a class insisted that students have their cameras on during meetings or presentations and that will be expected of them and standard in business in their futures. On the other hand, I've had clients who were clearly a challenge. For example, the demands on my time and students surpassed the value of the points and experience.

Ultimately, for educators who are interested in integrating client projects in their courses, there are many ways to develop partnerships with clients. Faculty and staff can begin by utilizing their existing university's connections and partnerships. In my experience, organizations have marketing challenges every day, and they are interested in finding students who can help them come up with interesting ideas and solutions.

CONCLUSION

If you think of EL as "learning by doing," that is a good start. It's also about applying some of the concepts students already know to real situations. I am a strong advocate of EL and like to offer opportunities for hands-on learning through experiences that complement or build upon my classes and coursework. Additionally, as a faculty advisor, I have found that EL inspires students to reflect on what they might want to do after graduation and what they don't want to do. Because EL activities like client projects and simulations leave such an impression on students, I have found that they will seek out jobs which are similar to the EL experience that they had in my courses. I find that EL can be incredibly flexible and can be tailored to any major or career interest. It accommodates diverse learning styles and preferences, whether they be Diverger, Assimilator, Converger, and Accommodator (Kolb, 1984). What matters most is the students' response to the experience.

Student feedback about EL contained in my teaching evaluations included "a chance to help me improve myself and my work"; "at first I had no idea what I was doing, but ultimately there was so much benefit…"; "it's all the interviewer wanted to talk about"; "this really gave me a confidence boost"; and "I'd love to see you do more of this and to do more in all classes." It will be so interesting to see what new models of EL emerge and how they can be incorporated into the classroom (or via Zoom). I will have to keep my eye on the EL ball.

REFERENCES

Auman, C. (2011). Using simulation games to increase student and instructor engagement. *College Teaching, 59*(4), 154–161. Retrieved March 26, 2021, from http://www.jstor.org/stable/41305132

Baker, D., Underwood, J., & Thakur, R. (2017). Factors contributing to cognitive absorption and grounded learning effectiveness in a competitive business marketing simulation. *Marketing Education Review, 27*(3), 127–140.

Concrete/Reflective/Abstract/Active – David Kolb. (n.d.). Retrieved March 22, 2021, from https://web.cortland.edu/andersmd/learning/kolb.htm

Cooke, L., & Williams, S. (2004). Two approaches to using client projects in the college classroom. *Business Communication Quarterly, 67*(2), 139–152.

Kolb, D. A. (1984). *Experiential learning: Experience as the source of learning and development.* Prentice-Hall.

Kolb, A. Y., & Kolb, D. A. (2005). *The Kolb learning style inventory – Version 3.1: 2005 technical specifications.* Hay Resources Direct.

Kolb, A., & Kolb, D. (2011). Experiential learning theory: A dynamic, holistic approach to management learning, education and development. In S. J. Armstrong & C. Fukami (Eds.), *Handbook of management learning, education and development.* https://doi.org/10.4135/9780857021038.n3

Kolb, A. Y., & Kolb, D. A. (2012). Experiential learning theory. In N. M. Seel (Ed.), *Encyclopedia of the sciences of learning.* Springer. https://doi.org/10.1007/978-1-4419-1428-6_227

Rooks, R. N., & Holliman B. D. (2018). Facilitating undergraduate learning through community-engaged problem-based learning. *International Journal for the Scholarship of Teaching and Learning, 12*(2). EBSCOhost, https://eds-s-ebscohost-com.libproxy.udayton.edu/eds/detail/detail?vid=0&sid=a9506760-c306-4245-aa94-ad0c31d9b656%40redis&bdata=JnNpdGU9ZWRzLWxpdmU%3d#db=eric&AN=EJ1186070

Tritsch, E. (2020). *Which are you? Accommodator, assimilator, converger, or diverger.* Retrieved March 26, 2021, from https://fairborndigital.us/2020/08/26/which-are-you-accommodator-assimilator-converger-or-diverger/

Udayton.edu. (2021). *School of Business Administration.* University of Dayton. [online] Available at: https://udayton.edu/business/landing-page-test.php. Accessed 30 Mar 2021.

Why study abroad? (2021). Retrieved U.S. Department of State on March 22, 2021, from https://studyabroad.state.gov/value-study-abroad/why-study-abroad

Why Teach with Simulations? (2020). Retrieved from Pedagogy in Action the SERC portal for Educators: https://serc.carleton.edu/sp/library/simulations/why.html

Experiential Learning in Laboratory Courses: Reflections on the Tiny Earth Curriculum

Yvonne Sun

What do you think about when you imagine science laboratory classes? Students wearing safety goggles holding flasks and beakers of colorful liquids? Students looking into microscopes? Students hiking outdoors collecting samples or performing different kinds of measurements? Yes, while science laboratory classes are inherently hands-on, qualifications of laboratory classes as experiential learning (EL) experiences might not be an automatic assumption. When laboratory classes focus on standardized behaviors and correct answers, they leave out the opportunities to engage learners beyond their hands. Yet how do we bring authentic EL experiences safely and feasibly into laboratory courses? What does that even look like? This chapter describes one specific example, the Tiny Earth curriculum, and how the curriculum creates an opportunity for students to choose, thereby affirming learners as stakeholders who are emotionally engaged with their decisions. The disjointed quest for correct answers is replaced with a continuous journey of explorations. By bringing *ownership*

Y. Sun (✉)
Biology, University of Dayton, Dayton, OH, USA
e-mail: ysun02@udayton.edu

K. Lovett (ed.), *Diverse Pedagogical Approaches to Experiential Learning, Volume II*,
https://doi.org/10.1007/978-3-030-83688-7_7

and *purpose* into laboratory experiences for students, the Tiny Earth curriculum ultimately and quite surprisingly provides a more authentic EL experience.

EXPERIENTIAL LEARNING IN SCIENCE LABORATORY CLASSES?

In natural sciences, learning by doing has been an integral part of the curriculum since the beginning of the disciplines. These learning activities can happen in laboratory settings in well-ventilated, temperature-controlled classroom spaces or out in the wild on land or waters. Students need to handle tools and learn techniques that are designed to help them prepare for careers where these skills are essential. Students are immersed in a working environment mimicking real-world work settings—from preparing for activities, executing procedures, to writing up the overall experiences. However, are these laboratory experiences qualified simply as active learning or EL?

The field of microbiology started because of individuals looking through carefully crafted lenses and investigating the tiny life forms that were once invisible to our naked eyes. Learning microbiology has always involved using our hands, eyes, and sometimes even noses to understand these invisible critters. Microbiology courses typically come with hands-on laboratory components where students learn how to cultivate microorganisms and use different microscopic, biochemical, and molecular tools by physically being in the lab and personally operating a microscope or spreading bacteria over a semi-solid agar surface. Students also need to write up lab reports to demonstrate their learning of not just the practical skills but also the rationale behind the application of these skills. The same question arises: aren't these laboratory activities de facto EL?

The six-step guide provided by the UD Office of Experiential Learning (n.d.) describes EL to include an "immerse" step where instructors "create opportunities for self-guided learning and experimentation," a "reflect" step where instructors "embed reflection activities before, during, and after the experience," a "connect" step where instructors "make connections and help students integrate and synthesize experiences," and an "apply" step where instructors "prepare students to take next steps with their experiential knowledge." These suggestions sound almost written to describe science laboratory classes! Students *immerse* in performing experiments, *reflect* on their experiments in their lab reports or lab notebooks, *connect* with their experiments by analyzing the results, and finally *apply* what they learn by interpreting their results.

As a laboratory instructor, can I declare myself an experiential learning practitioner?

BIOLOGY CURRICULUM AT THE UNIVERSITY OF DAYTON

All biology majors at UD are required to take a variety of laboratory courses, including four semesters of chemistry labs, two semesters of physics labs, and ten semesters of biology labs. For bean-counting purposes, if each laboratory class offers lab experiences for 3 hours per week in a 15-week long semester, these add up to a total of 720 hours of lab work, or the equivalent of 18 weeks of a full-time job. This number doesn't take into account the amount of time students spend outside of the class reading and preparing for labs, writing up reports, or studying for assessments. Moreover, many students go above and beyond these courses and pursue additional laboratory experiences in faculty research labs. Therefore, all our major graduates essentially have completed a full semester of co-op experience in science laboratories. If laboratory classes are a true form of EL, then our students have been receiving an intensive series of experiential learning across multiple disciplines!

To take a logistical look at typical science laboratory classes, we deploy a large instructional force and a substantial amount of financial and infrastructure support to accommodate a large number of students. For example, BIO 411L General Microbiology Lab, offered at 16 students per section and 9 sections per year, can cost up to $25,000 in materials and supplies plus 1–2 part-time undergraduate student workers on an annual basis. The behind-the-scenes support, from waste disposal to equipment maintenance and material receiving and delivering, likely adds to the price tag and the effort necessary to support the laboratory courses as part of the required component in our curriculum. For field-based laboratory classes, additional transportation requirements and communications with community partners demand even more extensive coordination.

In a typical setting, science laboratory classes are linked to the corresponding lecture classes to provide the opportunity for students to be deeply engaged with the concepts they are learning. For example, when students are learning about the concepts of certain reactions in lectures, they get to perform and witness the reactions taking place, thereby experiencing the temperature or color changes of these reactions. The sensory stimuli, together combined with conceptual understanding, create the full learning experiences to consolidate the integration of a new idea. However, because of deficiency in space and resources, many laboratory courses in the Department of Biology at UD are offered separately at a lower capacity insufficient to accommodate all the students enrolled in the corresponding lecture course. This numerical discrepancy, however frustration-inducing for many students, is the norm throughout the department. As a result, it is very common for students to take the lecture and laboratory courses in separate semesters, thereby compromising the pedagogical goal of linking hands-on learning opportunities with lecture materials. Does this disconnect compromise the qualification of laboratory courses as EL? Is it possible to create authentic EL in laboratory courses without the intensive corresponding lectures?

Moreover, in order to recapitulate real-world work environments, laboratory courses have inherent safety risks from outdoor fieldwork to indoor handling of toxic materials. To ensure the safety of a large number of students, strict safety plans and numerous safety trainings are necessary. These safety concerns also inevitably influence curricular designs. Students are often asked to follow specific experimental procedures, arriving at identical results, because deviations from the protocol or curiosity for alternative methods can be dangerous for novice practitioners. For a Biology major student going through 16 laboratory courses in the degree program, following step-by-step instructions in the lab is the expected behavior like adhering to the measurements of all ingredients in a recipe. If all the procedures and outcomes are predetermined and uniform, how do we make EL more personal and authentic for students in these laboratory courses?

Introduction of the Tiny Earth Curriculum

To provide perhaps some answers to all these questions, I want to share the story of one particular laboratory course at the UD. The BIO 411L General Microbiology Lab is a highly demanded course that has expanded quite significantly since 2014 when I arrived at UD. However, with the publisher losing rights to the lab manual and with the faculty member retiring, a curricular emergency suddenly emerged, demanding us to quickly identify suitable replacement materials. I was reminded of a talk by Dr. David H. Gorski where he described how his Hippocratic Oath to do no harm motivated him to take actions on vaccine literacy. Because not taking action, in this case, was him doing harm. Although my PhD degree did not come with a similar oath, I was compelled to take actions that could have a positive impact on the world. As a pre-tenure faculty armed with nothing other than naivety and idealistic visions, I decided to go outside of my comfort zone and shoot for the moon.

I proposed the introduction of a course-based undergraduate research (CURE) model for BIO 411L to the department chair at that time, who immediately offered his wholehearted support. In Summer 2018, I was supported by the department and received a week-long training at the University of Connecticut on an internationally recognized program—Tiny Earth (Hurley et al., 2021). In Fall 2018, under the advice of the new department chair, a graduate student and I piloted the curriculum to a small cohort of 9 students, which was expanded to 1 full section of 15 students in Spring 2019 and then to all sections starting Fall 2019.

The main mission for Tiny Earth is to strengthen the development of a diverse STEM workforce and to address the global issue of antimicrobial resistance. Briefly, STEM education is often delivered in an intensively content-centered manner for its efficiency as an information delivery system from an instructor to a typically large classroom of students. Standardized testing is the traditional method of assessment, which takes on the form of a "practicum" in laboratory courses where students rotate through stations and answer questions within the allotted time at each station. This pedagogical approach is well known to disadvantage underrepresented students (Theobald et al., 2020) thereby hampering the effort to enhance the diversity of the STEM workforce. As a separate but related issue, antimicrobial resistance, the phenomenon of microbial pathogens developing resistance to available antibiotic treatments, creates a global threat to modern medicine and basic human rights to healthcare. The World Health Organization has dedicated one week in November every year since 2015 as the World Antimicrobial Awareness Week to help raise global awareness of the antimicrobial resistance issue (Tiny Earth Network, 2020). This complicated issue requires interdisciplinary solutions and collaborations that can be supported by a diverse STEM workforce.

To accomplish the mission, Tiny Earth recruited instructors across the educational landscape, from K-12, community college, and 4-year universities, to deliver a laboratory curriculum as a CURE to engage students in authentic antibiotic discovery research. What began by Dr. Jo Handelsman in 2012 at Yale University has blossomed into a global network of 350 institutions, training over 10,000 students since the establishment of Tiny Earth Network in June 2016 (World Health Organization, n.d.). Besides training partner instructors, Tiny Earth organizes regular symposiums and workshop series to deeply engage all participating students and instructors, thereby creating an amazing and well-connected learning community.

A more direct comparison between the Tiny Earth curriculum and a traditional microbiology laboratory course is listed in Table 7.1 below. Students in a traditional microbiology laboratory learn a variety of fundamental laboratory skills for the majority of the semester using bacteria provided by the instructor to make sure their techniques are accurate and results are consistent. These skills are then put into use toward the end of the semester where students are given an unknown organism, typically one they've already worked with before, and are asked to determine the identity of the organism. There is a correct answer that is known to the instructor that students must arrive to receive full credit for the assessment.

In contrast, the Tiny Earth curriculum starts with unknown organisms that students collect based on their own choice of sampling location and

Table 7.1 A comparison between the traditional and Tiny Earth microbiology laboratory weekly schedules

Week	Traditional	Tiny Earth
1	Lab safety	Lab safety
2	Aseptic techniques	Soil collection, aseptic technique[a], and spread plate
3	Streak/spread plates	Streak plate[a]
4	Gram staining	Antibiotic susceptibility testing[a]
5	*Growth curve lab report*	Gram stain[a]
6	Selective and differential media	Selective and differential media
7	Selective and differential media	Biochemical testing[a]
8	Biochemical testing	Biochemical testing
9	Biochemical testing	16s rRNA PCR
10	Antibiotic susceptibility testing	Gel electrophoresis[a]
11	*Practicum*	Chemical extraction
12	Identification of unknown bacteria	Chemical extraction
13	Identification of unknown bacteria	Efficacy and toxicity testing
14	*Final lab report & exam*	*Final story*

Note. The italicized items are part of the course assessments

[a]Marks the skillset that is assessed in the following week after the introduction of the skills. The electronic lab notebook for the Tiny Earth curriculum, not shown in the table, is also assessed for a total of four times throughout the semester, three times by the instructor, and once by peers

enrichment media. Students are asked to describe why and how they choose the location. Students are asked to research the four different media types that are offered by the course, pick two, and describe their rationale for the selection. This decision-making step that takes place at the very beginning of the semester helps build the ownership into the curriculum. Students know where their bacterial isolates came from, such as the spot where their neighbors tend to vomit in, or the goals behind choosing the media types, such as the desire to see specific types of microbes. Most importantly, the instructors have no knowledge of the identity of these isolates and will now have to take the same journey with the students to discover what these isolates are and what they can do. When the instructor introduces a variety of skills and tools to guide the students in identifying the unknown isolates and testing for their antibiotic production activity, both parties are invested in finding out the answers and overcoming the obstacles along the way.

STUDENTS: THE TINY EARTHLINGS

Students in the Tiny Earth curriculum isolate bacteria from soil samples of their choice and test the isolates for antibiotic productions in a semester-long laboratory course. They learn basic microbiology techniques to characterize and analyze their own bacterial isolates with their instructors acting as research mentors. Instructors are no longer just delivering information and monitoring for safe behavior in the lab. They are actively engaged in training students in performing proper techniques and helping them interpret their results. When a student arrives at a finding, the instructor and the student both work to come up with interpretations. When a student makes a mistake, the instructor and the student work together to identify the source of the mistake and the appropriate steps to correct the mistakes. Because each student works with their own isolates, despite the procedural conformity, they all arrive at different outcomes. The joy and excitement when the isolates were seen under the microscopes were felt by instructors and their students.

The sense of ownership is deeply felt by all the students in BIO 411L with the Tiny Earth curriculum. Besides working to a Spotify collaborative playlist populated by songs of their choice, students are working with bacteria isolated from a location of their choice, using media types chosen after performing their own research. They test for antibiotic production activity using target organisms chosen after performing their own research.

By simply having opportunities to choose, students become emotionally invested in taking care of their isolates and are eager to learn about different ways to get to know their isolates. They are fully aware of and excited about the progression of the labs. They are frustrated when their experiments do not work. They are sad when they have to throw their isolates away at the end of the semester. Ultimately, the students become the stakeholders in their learning and practicing of fundamental laboratory skills in a carefully created learning environment where they are the decision-makers and the executioners.

We also replace standardized testing with skill set assessments. Students need to demonstrate their mastery of fundamental microbiology laboratory skills by doing them, repeatedly if necessary, correctly. For example, a Gram staining skill assessment requires students to prepare a specimen for staining, perform the staining, visualize the stained specimen, and correctly interpret the staining result. If they make a mistake, like all of us in the real research setting do, they repeat the process until they master the technique. What sounds like a brutal boot camp exercise turns out to be a welcoming and more effective alternative to the students. Despite the initial frustration, students in general appreciate the opportunities to repeat and truly learn the skills. Many express confidence in their skills even months after the semester is over!

The sense of ownership over their work and the confidence in their skills together instill—using a word mentioned by many students—*purpose* to their learning. Instead of fragmented and independent lessons, the entire semester is one cohesive journey for these Tiny Earthlings and their instructors.

Outcomes and Findings

When we forego the traditional quest for correct answers, we witness in the Tiny Earth students an amazing array of creativity. To demonstrate skill set mastery, students were asked to make videos of them performing the tasks using common household items. For example, students made videos demonstrating the process of streaking plates, a basic skill of isolating single colonies on agar, by spreading butter over a lid with a knife. They made videos of serial dilution using colorful beverages or "cereal," pun intended. They made videos of the Gram staining procedure with acrylic paints. To create the final presentation, students have made animated videos featuring themselves as the scientist or their isolates as a bachelor contestant. They have made Instagram and Twitter accounts for their isolates to tell the discovery and characterization story. All of these creative outcomes demonstrate their learning and their full engagement with their learning. Moreover, they help motivate the instructors who can now provide feedback to student learning without making the same comments on dozens of similarly written lab reports.

Because of the gradual rollout of this new curriculum, we had a unique opportunity to have concurrent traditional and Tiny Earth sections to explore and compare the impact of the different formats on the students. When we compared the informal feedback of students from either a traditional 411L or the 411L using the Tiny Earth curriculum, several differences were noted. While the traditional students only encountered challenges at the end of the semester when they had to identify an "unknown" organism, Tiny Earth students faced challenges in the lab throughout the semester when learning different techniques and had the opportunities to practice and correct them with instructor feedback. Because many of the biochemical tests were designed for clinical diagnostic purposes, when used for soil microbes, they often generate results that don't perfectly fit the prescribed outcomes of these tests. These often stimulate additional discussions among instructors and students and demand a higher level of critical thinking skill.

While the traditional students qualified the two lab reports as demonstrating their analytical and narrative reasoning skills, the Tiny Earth students offered a variety of more examples, from maintaining their electronic lab notebooks throughout the semester to making multiple informed decisions in their research progress and the preparation and the delivery of their final research presentations. Tiny Earth students in the Spring semester also have the additional advantage of presenting at the campus-wide student research symposium or the Tiny Earth Summer symposium to share their findings. Moreover, Tiny Earth students have adopted a variety of presentation formats beyond the traditional written report or slide-based presentation, ranging from Instagram posts, children's storybooks to animation videos.

While traditional students considered interactions with their peers during class time as encountering diverse perspectives, Tiny Earth students provided a wider range of situations, from diversity of their soil isolates to in-class discussions with other students, research presentations, and peer-evaluations of electronic notebooks. The interactions between instructors and students throughout the semester are also rewarding to the instructors. The graduate instructors have the opportunity to practice their skills as research mentors who can guide the students instead of just providing answers. The connections between the course, the instructor, and the students are much richer and diverse in the Tiny Earth curriculum than the traditional curriculum.

Human experiences are deeply linked to our emotions. While traditional students don't recognize any emotional engagement, Tiny Earth students experience a wider range of emotions. These emotional engagements, from excitement to frustration, fuel their actions and learning. The emotional exhibitions from the students speak not only to the safety of the learning environment but also to the course as an authentic learning experience for the students.

Personal Reflections

All the laboratory classes I remember taking as a student had correct answers. There was a correct name for a bird, an invertebrate, or a plant. There was a correct terminology for a structure. There was a correct volume of solution we needed to use. There was a correct number for a calculation. However complex and dynamic the learning was, taking place indoor or outdoor, everything had a correct answer. We trained our hands and the rest of our learning machinery to reach that correct answer so we gained, at the minimum, the safety awareness around toxic and dangerous materials and hopefully also the technical language and skills to communicate and generate new and useful knowledge. That was the EL I had and was one of the contributing reasons I favored certain disciplines over others.

After my experiences with delivering the Tiny Earth curriculum, I can't help but look back at the traditional microbiology laboratory courses, which have remained largely unchanged since I was an undergraduate student, and wonder whether science laboratory courses are truly by definition a form of EL. If the traditional class offers a quest for correct answers, the Tiny Earth curriculum is a journey to explore. At the end of the day, the students are learning mostly the same techniques following either of the formats. However, the sense of ownership, purpose, and confidence is much more evident in students when they have the opportunities to explore. By having opportunities to make decisions, students take on decision-making roles. By having opportunities to make mistakes and correct those mistakes, students develop resilience and acceptance to feedback. By participating in a continuous, project-based learning experience, students develop stronger connections between the different skill sets. By having a real-world issue and the rise of antimicrobial resistance, students find meaning and motivation in what they are learning.

All these additional benefits that I've been witnessing make me realize that while the traditional laboratory courses are certainly designed for EL, acquiring the benefits of EL experiences is not a guaranteed outcome and can be highly learner-dependent. If students don't come already equipped with motivation and passion, their perceptions of learning change. Fieldwork becomes manual labor. Writing lab reports becomes a time-consuming chore. Microbiology research becomes a simple, meaningless act of transferring small amounts of liquids. While performing manual labor, completing a time-consuming chore, or transferring small amounts of liquids can certainly allow a student to pass and excel in a laboratory course, mastery over these tasks doesn't translate to a fully engaged student.

There is almost a sacred bond between instructors and courses they painstakingly develop. And the pride and exhilaration that come from a course that works as designed keep us addicted to what we do. For this course specifically, I have witnessed perfectionist students go from struggling with facing their mistakes to openly admitting their need for help. I have seen students expressing curiosity and the action being enthusiastically taken to address their curiosity. I have watched unbelievably creative videos of students sharing their laboratory skills using common household items and their final stories where they summarize their journeys of discovery. By completely trusting this new pedagogical approach, Tiny Earth students, regardless of their GPAs or experiences, become engaged and invested learners. Stopping by the laboratory classes while students are working is often the highlight of my day!

The final point to mention is the network of Tiny Earth Partner Instructors, or TEPIs as we call ourselves. I've helped organize monthly workshops to provide forums for TEPIs to share ideas and as a result have learned new ways to improve my own course. Moreover, these regular interactions with other instructors have helped me realize the fluidity and modularity of the Tiny Earth curriculum. While we are delivering a full, semester-long curriculum, we can easily take parts of the curriculum and use them for community outreach activities or in other interdisciplinary education programs so that the opportunity to choose and explore is abundantly available for the students as well as the instructors. There is a community available to support each other's explorations and creativities and to reflect on each other's reflections. At the end of the day, our students are not the only ones having the EL experience, us instructors do too. And I think that makes me an EL practitioner and the course a true EL opportunity.

REFERENCES

Hurley, A., Chevrette, M. G., Acharya, D. D., Lozano, G. L., Garavito, M., Heinritz, J., Balderrama, L., Beebe, M., DenHartog, M. L., Corinaldi, K., Engels, R., Gutierrez, A., Jona, O., Putnam, J. H. I., Rhodes, B., Tsang, T., Hernandez, S., Bascom-Slack, C., Blum, J. E., ... Handelsman, J. (2021). Tiny Earth: A big idea for STEM education and antibiotic discovery. *MBio, 12*. https://doi.org/10.1128/mBio.03432-20

Theobald, E. J., Hill, M. J., Tran, E., Agrawal, S., Arroyo, E. N., Behling, S., Chambwe, N., Cintrón, D. L., Cooper, J. D., Dunster, G., Grummer, J. A., Hennessey, K., Hsiao, J., Iranon, N., Jones, L., Jordt, H., Keller, M., Lacey, M. E., Littlefield, C. E., ... Freeman, S. (2020). Active learning narrows achievement gaps for underrepresented students in undergraduate science, technology, engineering, and math. *Proceedings of the National Academy of Sciences of the United States of America, 117*(12), 6476–6483. https://doi.org/10.1073/pnas.1916903117

Tiny Earth Network. (2020). *Our Network.* https://tinyearth.wisc.edu/about-us/our-network/

University of Dayton Office of Experiential Learning. (n.d.). *Experiential learning: 6 step guide for EL practitioners at UD.* UDayton.edu. https://udayton.edu/el/faculty-staff-resources/index.php

World Health Organization. (n.d.). *World antimicrobial awareness week.* https://www.who.int/campaigns/world-antimicrobial-awareness-week

Race, Gender, Faith, and Cross-Cultural Perspectives in Experiential Learning

Leveraging Experiential Learning to Create Inclusive Community at Predominantly White Institutions

Castel Sweet, Tom Morgan, and Jesse Hughes

The University of Dayton (UD) was founded in 1850 as the St. Mary's school for boys, and 70 years later would assume the identity that it maintains today. UD is a Catholic Marianist institution that centers its values of education around faith, service, and community. The UD undergraduate student body consists of approximately 8000 full-time students on average, 79% to 80% of whom identified as white from 2019 to 2020,

C. Sweet
Center for Community Engagement, University of Mississippi,
Oxford, MS, USA
e-mail: cvsweet@olemiss.edu

T. Morgan (✉)
English, University of Dayton, Dayton, OH, USA
e-mail: tmorgan2@udayton.edu

J. Hughes
Biology, University of Dayton, Dayton, OH, USA
e-mail: hughesj7@udayton.edu

K. Lovett (ed.), *Diverse Pedagogical Approaches to Experiential Learning, Volume II*,
https://doi.org/10.1007/978-3-030-83688-7_8

qualifying the university as a predominantly white institution (PWI). It has been shown that the campus racial climate at a PWI can have significant effects on the overall success and retention of students of color (Hurtado et al., 1999). Students of color that attend PWIs often are faced with structural racism that remains within the institution as a result of not addressing its past indiscretions pertaining to racial exclusivity, along with macro- and microaggressions from members of the university's larger community.

As a Marianist institution, the UD's values are aligned with a commitment to the work of Diversity, Equity, and Inclusion, but often we fall short of making this commitment a practical reality. In addition to facing the challenges of the rigorous coursework that is required of UD students, students of color must navigate their higher education experience with the challenges that accompany attending an institution that is still reckoning with the racial injustices of the past. These challenges range from the seemingly minute (racially charged graffiti in public spaces) to institutionally engrained (harassment from campus police). Such incidents take a toll on the psychological health of our students of color, which may lead them to leave their education behind. The issues discussed above provide a case for why it is necessary to empower our students, in particular students of color, to advocate for themselves and provide them with the resources and connections that are needed to create change in their institutions of higher learning.

In response, Creating Inclusive Community (CIC) was established to cultivate a sustainable infrastructure that fosters ongoing conversations on privilege in all its forms and uses experiential learning (EL) to encourage and facilitate sustainable action steps toward greater social justice on campus and beyond. By exposing participants to an established diversity and social justice curriculum as well as a subsequent off-campus conference experience, CIC provides a safe space to interact with groups of people that UD students might not normally interact with. This chapter will focus on the processes involved in designing and implementing this EL experience which aims to develop understanding, respect, and connection among students.

Instigated in early 2015 by a faculty member interested in coordinating a group of university faculty, staff, and students to attend the White Privilege Conference being held in 2016 in Louisville, Kentucky, CIC was originally imagined as a voluntary collaborative effort intended to provide students exposure and engagement with diversity-based dialogue skills intended to promote inclusivity on campus. Currently, CIC is overseen by a core team composed of a rotating convener and representatives from a variety of campus units including student development, academic affairs and learning initiatives, college of arts and sciences, and school of business. Each member of the core team is expected to contribute in some form to the advancement of the goals and/or outcomes of the initiative. The work is organized into three subgroups and led by a core group which has a representative from each of the four areas. Over the five years, CIC has been institutionally supported by a Graduate Assistant to help coordinate programming and travel, a course release for the faculty member teaching the mini-course, and funding for the conference experience and fall action project.

The CIC model operates on the calendar year, and combines the curricular and co-curricular into a structure that leverages EL to achieve diversity and social justice learning outcomes that can impact the institution broadly. During the spring term, a cohort of participants are enrolled in the dialogue-based course, travel to the conference together, deliver a campus-wide presentation, and begin developing an action plan for a fall project. In the fall term, the cohort refines and implements its spring action plan. In addition to the cohort experience, CIC offers ongoing engagement for past, current, or future participants in the form of article discussions, book reads, and group dialogues on current events and topics. Given the unique nature of this initiative and the UD's mini-course model, we have outlined various challenges, successes, and lessons learned regarding the structuring and implementation of this EL program. We aim to provide insights relating to identified strengths and weaknesses when empowering students to pursue social justice work at predominantly white institutions.

This chapter will feature personal reflections from individuals involved in the Creating Inclusive Community initiative. Tom Morgan, Associate Professor of American and African-American Literature and current Director of the Race and Ethnic Studies Program, served five years as the faculty facilitator for the spring mini-course experience, and has been a member of the CIC Core Team since the beginning. Jesse Hughes, a chemistry doctoral student, was a part of the first CIC cohort as an undergraduate student before beginning his graduate work at UD, and has been a teacher's assistant for the spring course ever since. Castel Sweet, Director of Community Engagement and Diversity, Equity, & Inclusion in the School of Business Administration, participated in the CIC 2018 Cohort, co-facilitated the 2019 and 2020 Cohorts, and currently serves as the convener of the CIC Core Team.

CHALLENGES DELIVERING A TRANSFORMATIONAL EL EXPERIENCE WITHIN RIGID STRUCTURES

With CIC being a unique initiative that crosses both curricular and co-curricular lines, the model comes with particular challenges. CIC mirror's Kolb's (1984) experiential learning style theory in which "learning is the process whereby knowledge is created through the transformation of experience (p. 38)". CIC guides students through Kolb's four-stage learning cycle by providing participants with a *concrete experience* traveling to a conference for practitioners who examine challenging concepts of privilege and oppression; facilitating *reflective observation* on participants' experience at the conference and their personal experiences with privilege and oppression; encouraging participants to *conceptualize* their learning from those experience; and supporting *active experimentation* by applying their learning through the development and execution of action plans to further address issues of inclusion on campus.

When conceptualized, CIC was intentionally developed as a cross-campus initiative that was not limited to one particular unit or department. Instead, student, staff, and faculty participants reflected the diversity of the campus in position, disciplines, and social identities. Even though this is one of the primary aspects of CIC that contributes to its impact, within the context of higher education that typically functions within departmental silos, the desired level of campus-wide collaboration can be difficult to implement within the given structures, especially considering that it does not have a formal home where the initiative is located. Except for a graduate assistant, the individuals who comprise the CIC Core Team volunteer their time to support the initiative. Without CIC being formally written into anyone's job description, ensuring broad campus representation is present often depends on the personal interests and investment of faculty and staff. This can often cause the core team to feel as if they are continuously advocating for the sustainability of the initiatives and the need for institutional resources.

Without being housed within an academic department, the course experience currently does not qualify to fulfill any degree requirements, although it is a credit bearing course. Despite being delivered in something of a traditional course format, the lack of specific academic requirements for the experience can potentially deter interested students from participating due to other degree priorities. This can be seen as a common treatment of particular types of nontraditional experiential learning opportunities, giving the impression that if the learning experience does not take place in the classroom or within certain parameters that it does not count. In conversation with administration, the CIC Core Team has discussed the possibility of housing CIC under both the Race and Ethnic Studies program and the Office of Diversity and Inclusion, however, the potential impact on the program structure to limit the participation of graduate students, staff, and faculty as members of the yearly cohort is less desirable. In fact, the additional barriers to inclusion could arguably be the antithesis of the initiative's original intent and purpose.

Identifying ways to facilitate transformational experiential learning opportunities within a rigid structure of higher education can be a challenge. Due to the various formats and experiences that take place during many EL offerings, traditional course models may not provide an adequate space to facilitate the desired activities to achieve the identified learning outcomes. However, the limitation of traditional academic courses should not hinder the ability for experiential learning offerings to be transcripted or satisfy academic requirements.

The current model of the program spans a calendar year, with the first part of the experience taking place during the spring semester and the second part during the subsequent fall semester. Identifying the course as distinct from traditional academic courses, many participants arrive at the first session with the expectation and desire to immediately engage in action. Being attracted to the initiative's EL aspect of the action project, some participants are initially taken aback to learn that the spring semester consists of developing dialogue skills and doing the self-work necessary to prepare for productive engagement across differences (Table 8.1).

Instead of spending the first part of the experience developing action projects, participants are guided through activities that will help them better understand themselves before they turn to learning about others. In order to truly be an agent of change, comprehension of social identities and how they influence social interactions and engagement across differences is foundational. Therefore, participants talk through notions of social identity, white privilege, and engage in group and personal reflections to help conceptualize how these concepts are manifested in our daily lives. Once participants are comfortable with these understandings, they

Table 8.1   Overview of spring mini-course schedule

Date	Goals	Objectives
Weeks 1–2	Class overview Individual identity: Who am I?	Build community within cohort Engage in self-reflection of identity Introduce social identity, power, and privilege
Weeks 3–5	Who are we? intersectionality, group identity, and conflict	Explore intergroup relationships Reflect on personal and group intersectionality Learn about the role of conflict
Weeks 6–9	Systematic inequality	Learn and reflect on social, political, and cultural structures Examine and understand the interaction between individual choices, group actions, and social structures
Weeks 10–12	Allyhood and coalition building	Reflect on role as an ally Begin planning fall project

are then able to apply what they have learned and discussed through identified action projects on campus.

The two part format was intentionally structured around the calendar year instead of the academic year since the conference is held in the spring, however, the summer break in between presents a test of participant retention with each cohort. While cohorts return from the conference inspired to share and apply all they have learned, the inspiration seems to dissipate during the summer months and the fire is often difficult to re-ignite for many once everyone has returned to campus the following fall. In addition, spring graduation initiates the dwindle of fall participant numbers. The return to campus in the fall signals the start of a new academic year, thus, previous spring initiatives and programs are often a thing of the past. Attending to reconvene the spring cohort to start implementing fall projects requires patience and understanding. In addition to students who do not return to campus as a result of graduation or other circumstances, there are also those who may not be able to commit due to other priorities. As a participant of the first CIC cohort, and a teacher's assistant to the subsequent six cohorts that follow, Jesse Hughes has witnessed the challenges of participant retention first hand:

In the multiple cohorts that I participated in over the years, there is a noticeable difference in student engagement over the summer between the first and second semesters. Something that I have observed as a factor for student engagement is the state of the national discourse on race. In moments of civil unrest throughout the country, where issues of racial justice are receiving national attention, people seem to be more engaged across semesters, and the retention from Spring to Fall is high. The opposite has been true in cohorts where there was no national conversation regarding racial justice over the summer between courses. It can be overwhelming as a student to balance course work, jobs, and any other responsibilities while also trying to advocate for institutional change at your university. In addition to trying to enact change, we must continue our personal education and growth to understand further the historical context of the injustices we seek to overcome. Handling all of these responsibilities might make it easier for a student to get distracted from the work they committed to in the previous semester.

Identifying consistent ways for staff and faculty in the cohort to contribute to the fall project has yet to be fully realized. The program is structured to be an experiential learning opportunity in which participants independently conceptualize their learning from the program, then actively experiment by applying that learning through an action project. Following the conference experience, participants are led through reflective dialogue about their participation in the conference, and through such dialogue identify ways to actionize their learning. Reflecting on the experience through dialogue with others in the cohort helps participants develop a multidimensional picture of the experience (Kolb, 1984), and ideally provides a foundation on which to develop an action project that not only would benefit CIC participants, but also would be impactful for the entire campus. Action projects participants have taken on include organizing dialogues between campus police and underrepresented students on campus to foster better community-police relations, an accessibility map of campus to display the ways campus is or is not accessible to all physical abilities, and many others. With the desire to ensure students feel empowered to create and have ownership of actualizing the campus and community they feel is needed, staff and faculty typically assume a secondary role in the planning and implementation of action projects. Oftentimes, taking a secondary role means faculty and staff are not engaged throughout the lifespan of the project and tend to slowly slip out of the frame. Understanding actions' projects for faculty and staff may look different from an action project designed by undergraduate and graduate students, identifying ways for the entire cohort to co-design and implement together while providing students with equitable empowerment is challenging. As a consistent co-instructor of the course for multiple semesters, Tom Morgan has firsthand experience with attempting to navigate such challenges of ensuring the program is an equitable experiential learning opportunity for all participants:

> *Developing realistic action plans with students, faculty, and staff has been one of the greater challenges we've faced. Much like in the spring mini-course, where participants immediately want to leap into action, fall participants regularly identify projects that could take years, if not decades, to accomplish. Focusing on projects that can be planned, organized, implemented, and accomplished in a semester has helped our participants think about the relationship between short-, medium-, and long-term planning as part of the process. The focus on what can be accomplished in this semester, even if there is a greater and ongoing plan, has helped to build concrete, action-based skills that participants can use moving forward. Some of the projects have involved creating a campus-wide conference similar to WPC to bring that message more directly to campus, examining disability-based accessibility issues on campus by creating a campus-wide map of where accessibility is a problem to present to administrators, and working with campus police to create stronger connections between police and students of color. Additionally, CIC participants have gone on to join the Diversity Peer Educators program, been involved in developing and reviewing the interculturalism goal in Student Development programming, and pursuing diversity, equity, and inclusion work as part of their professional life once they left campus.*

Similarly, developing a full cohort experience starting with the dialogue-based course that includes all competency and awareness levels is not an easy feat. Being able to engage multiple audiences and various learning styles in a manner that is impactful and transformative as the desired outcomes requires a delicate sensitivity and consistent intentionality. There were times when participants were prepared and expected to dive deep into certain conversations, however, being mindful not to lose or push away participants who may still need foundational understandings caused inconsistent experiences throughout the course. The make-up and social identity of the cohort also greatly impacted the overall experiences. While participants of underrepresented groups sensed the dialogues as a safe space to articulate their experience with oppression, participants of privileged groups may have perceived this space as one that did not require their input. Even though this provides a challenge with engaging all participants and hearing all perspectives during group discussions, it also serves as a different type of learning experience for many participants.

Being aware of how we share conversation time with voices who may not be heard as often while still being inclusive of all identities can be tough to navigate. However, being able to practice intergroup dialogue within a learning community is a key component of the CIC experience. It is a practice and skill that can be applied to many facets of our lived experiences, one that extends well beyond our participation time together in the program.

ACTIVELY CREATING A SPACE CONDUCIVE FOR EL

Now in our sixth year, many lessons have been learned on how to accomplish the goals and objectives of CIC. With a desire to create and model more inclusive communities, notions of positionality are even more influential in the way they are performed and reinforced within the context of the experience. The individuals who serve as the two facilitators of each cohort are intentionally identified to be one faculty and one staff. Being co-facilitated by a faculty and a staff not only helps to connect the curricular to the co-curricular component of the program, but also illustrates the collaborative nature of the initiative and the shared ownership the entire campus must have to truly create a culture of inclusion across the campus. Additionally, selecting facilitators along with different intersectional identities like race and gender when possible can help strengthen engagement within individual cohorts by foregrounding the experience across perspectives that are the basis of this work. While the facilitators are formally documented as instructors for the course, over time we have identified that the best facilitators are previous participants in the class experience with the cohort and to serve as a guide only when needed.

We followed the University of Michigan Intergroup Dialogue model (Maxwell et al., 2011) of pairing facilitators across multiple aspects of identity, and using that to help build a deeper engagement with those participating. While creating a non-hierarchical space for engagement, one that includes undergraduate and graduate students, faculty, and staff, can be difficult, the ongoing pursuit of fostering that work has also been one of the most rewarding experiences during our time at UD. Early on, it was difficult for facilitators to remember the need to de-center their own experiences or identities, but as time went on, it became part of the daily practice of the course. And as previous students repeated the course as co-facilitators, that type of engagement became ingrained in the ethos of the course and the practices we collectively pursued. It also reflected the ways in with CIC served as an EL experience for the facilitators as well as the participants.

The conference added a very distinctive experience for participants. Not only is the White Privilege Conference unlike other academic conferences participants may be familiar with, but also the White Privilege Conference attracts a mosaic of attendees that spans from high school to retirees, academics to community activists and artists. It also spans the range of races, ethnicities, cultures, and genders. Attending the conference allowed cohort participants to learn new skills by further engaging in dialogue with diverse perspectives that may not be readily available on campus. It exposed the cohort to new languages and approaches used by others in conversations around privilege and oppression to identify ways to work toward equity and social justice. In addition, traveling together served as a community-building exercise that allowed the cohort to connect on a deeper level and bond as a group. The resulting cohesion and trust provided a beneficial foundation for the cohort to begin conceptualizing their action plan once they returned from the conference, and solidified the relationships needed to implement the fall project. As a participant of the first CIC cohort, Jessie Hughes describes his experience identifying and implementing a fall project with his peers.

After returning from the White Privilege Conference (WPC) for the first time as a cohort, reentering campus life was somewhat a shock for the students who participated in the CIC class. We returned to campus on St. Patrick's Day to a barrage of questions from our confused peers, "where have you been the last few days? What is this class? Why would they take you to a white power conference?" After trying to explain this experience to our fellow students, we realized that it would be better to bring something similar to it on campus to experience themselves. Three other members of my cohort and I began to construct a proposal outlining our vision for an on-campus conference experience that captured the essence of our time at the WPC. After a few months of planning, fundraising, and networking, we launched the first "Creating Inclusive Community Presents:" conference, including a morning and afternoon of concurrent sessions (each ending with time for affinity group caucusing) and an evening plenary keynote.

Leveraging EL and Collaborations to Create a More Inclusive Community

Despite the challenges of not having a department or unit home on campus, the collective approach of CIC has provided a de-hierarchical and de-siloed approach of leveraging EL to create and engage diversity and inclusion at a predominately white institution. Having support from a variety of campus stakeholders created a stronger network of support that elevates the reach, value, and impact of experiential learning initiatives (Smith and Betts, 2000), and this is illustrated through CIC's collective model. The decentralized collaboration also allows the initiative to incorporate a deeper connection for vocation exploration. By not being connecting to a particular department or course of study, participants aren't predisposed to associate the work from the confinements of a particular subject, but instead are encouraged to view the experience more holistically and to conceptualize how the work connects to their personal journey, calling, and desired life's work. Serving as the convener of the CIC Core Team, Castel Sweet shares her experience working collaboratively with others across campus to create a more inclusive community:

> *Working with faculty and staff across campus on this initiative has truly been one of the highlights of my experiences in higher education. We have individuals who represent academic departments as well as student development units. The diversity of the team itself really helps to cultivate a more holistic experience that is more capable of creating a truly inclusive community. This work does not fit into one particular campus unit or department, therefore those who are supporting the work shouldn't either. Being able to come together regardless of where we fall on the campus organizational chart, it really helps to embed this work into the campus in ways that aren't possible if led by a particular unit.*

One of the best ways we learned to build connection and coherence as a group was through journaling. Participants were periodically asked to write short journal entries for submission in class, where they focused on observing the world around them and thinking through the actions and behaviors they saw in their daily lives. In our weekly meetings, we spent time-sharing observations, and using these prompts as a way to talk about and discuss different responses to the events and experiences that different people shared with the group. The preparation ahead of time allowed everyone to gather stronger, more specific details, and also helped create the confidence to share from a feeling of being prepared. This sharing also helped build group trust through the conversations that emerged from individual observations, and offered a way to foreground the value of group dialogue as a means for collective awareness and growth.

Being able to leverage experiential learning to encourage and facilitate sustainable action steps toward greater social justice on campus and beyond has been critical to the success of the program. CIC has provided both participants and facilitators the opportunity to engage in a concrete experience, reflective observation, conceptualization of learning and facilitate active experimentation. By providing a space for participants to practice diversity work and develop their own abilities in a hands-on, practical, and active way, we encourage intentional engagement across intersectional differences and facilitate trust-building as part of creating our own community. These practices give all of us new skills to take with us out into the other groups and communities we engage on the campus, and have been instrumental in the growth and development of related initiatives elsewhere on campus. Similarly, students as well as faculty and staff have taken these skills with them when they left UD, intentionally choosing to continue this work in both their personal and professional lives. As Chapman, McPhee, and Proudman (1995) observe in "What Is Experiential Education?," "The experiential methodology is not linear, cyclical, or even patterned. It is a series of working principles, all of which are equally important" (p. 243). Learning to enact social justice as a daily practice requires both space and time to become familiar with the push and pull of these principles. Creating Inclusive Community has become our means to embody those principles.

REFERENCES

Chapman, S., McPhee, P., & Proudman, B. (1995). What is experiential education. In K. Warren (Ed.), *The theory of experiential education* (pp. 235–248). Kendall/Hunt Publishing Company.

Hurtado, S., Milem, J. F., Clayton-Pedersen, A., & Allen, W. (1999). *Enacting diverse learning environments: Improving the climate for racial/ethnic diversity in higher education institutions* (ASHE-ERIC higher education report series). George Washington University Graduate School of Education.

Kolb, D. A. (1984). *Experiential learning: Experience as the source of learning and development*. Prentice-Hall.

Maxwell, K., Nagda, B., & Chesler, M. (2011). Identity matters: Facilitators' struggles and empowered use of social identities in intergroup dialogue. In K. Maxwell, B. Nagda, & M. Thompson (Eds.), *Facilitating intergroup dialogues: Bridging differences, catalyzing change* (pp. 163–177). Stylus Publishing.

Smith, R., & Betts, M. (2000). Learning as partners: Realising the potential of work-based learning. *Journal of Vocational Education and Training, 52*(4), 589–604.

CHAPTER 9

393 Guineas: A Dialogue on Experiential Learning and Feminist Theory

David J. Fine and Mary McLoughlin

How does one teach for change? Clayton et al. (2014), for their part, challenge educators to walk the talk of democracy. In particular, they call for experiential learning (EL) projects that engage "students as *actors* in rather than *audience* of their own education" (p. 5). Clayton and her co-authors identify several strategies to achieve this shift. This chapter focuses on two: designing for power-sharing and designing for counter-normativity. If, as the authors write, "we seek to make power dynamics visible, to design inclusive processes that avoid ignoring or marginalizing anyone's contributions, and to reflect critically on the causes, consequences, and alternatives of and to enshrined systems of power" (p. 25), then "we must encourage the design of experiential learning in ways that are intentionally

D. J. Fine (✉)
English, University of Dayton, Dayton, OH, USA
e-mail: dfine1@udayton.edu

M. McLoughlin
Political Science, Syracuse University, Syracuse, NY, USA
e-mail: mmclough@syr.edu

© The Author(s), under exclusive license to Springer Nature
Switzerland AG 2022
K. Lovett (ed.), *Diverse Pedagogical Approaches to Experiential
Learning, Volume II*,
https://doi.org/10.1007/978-3-030-83688-7_9

disruptive and highlight, problematize, and offer democratic alternatives" (p. 27). In the account that follows, a student and teacher critically reflect on their different experiences of an "intentionally disruptive" EL project incorporated into Feminist Theory and Methodology (WGS 310). This reflection grounds an argument for counter-normative EL within feminist classrooms. In these spaces, students and teachers alike question what it means to do well at tasks not designed for justice and learn how to fail in pursuit of impossible—though valuable—goals.

Kolb (1984) underscores transformative experience's importance in student learning, and this chapter brings his foundational account to feminist pedagogy. At its best, EL expands students' education beyond university walls and—when paired with feminist theory that challenges patriarchal values and institutional hierarchies—provides an opportunity for all learners to interrogate internalized norms of higher education. While traditional education often prepares students to succeed within an unequable system, feminist EL makes room for failure within that system by introducing counter-normative values and goals. To clarify this shift, the opening section establishes EL's value for feminist pedagogy and describes the project integrated into WGS 310. This EL project, inspired by Woolf (1938), asks students to discern how best to spend funding in order to promote feminism. This task mirrors the dilemma at *Three Guineas'* core: Woolf's speaker, faced with structural injustice and escalating violence, must decide what to do with her money, too. After a description of the EL component, the second section breaks with scholarly convention, and the co-authors enter into dialogue. This conversation, modeled after hooks (1994), highlights the centrality of vigilant reflection to feminist EL, while taking seriously power differences among participants. The third section concludes with a summary of lessons unlearned.

FEMINIST PEDAGOGY

In *Teaching to Transgress*, hooks stresses the importance of active learning and shared power within progressive education. She writes that, in democratic classrooms, "a feeling of community creates a sense that there is shared commitment and a common good that binds us. What we ideally share is the desire to learn—to receive actively knowledge that enhances our intellectual development and our capacity to live more fully in the world" (p. 40). And yet, the norms of higher education often work against these ideals by prioritizing expert knowledge that disempowers students and community members (Saltmarsh et al., 2009). To be a feminist, how-ever, is to be committed to rejecting inequality in all its forms, especially when naturalized within institutions of higher education. Equipped with theory and committed to praxis, the feminist learner asks: What systems of power are creating inequity within and outside the classroom? What might education look like instead? How can feminists work toward that vision? EL sharpens these questions by giving them real-life stakes and develops, in turn, the practical skills necessary to address them. This chapter puts forward feminist EL, then, as one means by which to democratize education.

Feminist pedagogy has historically emphasized the link between theory and practice. Given this emphasis on critical reflection and lived experi-ence, EL enhances feminist pedagogy, allowing educators "to facilitate understanding of the context of one's own life and the lives of others, and to think about action as grounded in theory" (Oxley & Ilea, 2015, p. 2). EL provides educators, moreover, with a means by which to trouble con-ventional hierarchies. As Meagher (2015) argues, feminist pedagogy "calls on instructors to engage students in ways that counter individualist as well as authoritarian teaching methodologies; it demands that students be colearners and take responsibility for their learning" (p. 150). Feminist educators can thus intentionally use EL to redistribute power among learners and to cultivate self-efficacy. This redistribution is essential, because—beyond just thinking about what it means to be a woman or a man—feminist theory helps students to see where the patriarchal roles of domination and submission lead to other relational inequalities. In mak-ing room for feminist EL, educators link students' educations on the way power functions in the world to a consideration of how it works much closer to home.

Project Overview

WGS 310's EL project aims to divvy up authority and to disrupt higher education's taken-for-granted hierarchies. For these reasons, the instruc-tor transfers a $500 EL grant to students at the beginning of the semester. Together, they must determine how to spend this funding—their, roughly, 393 guineas—in order to promote feminism in the local community. This charge places students in the position of Woolf's letter-writer in *Three Guineas*. In her classic feminist essay, Woolf considers how women should employ the power and influence that come with their newfound financial independence to prevent war, even if their efforts are "doomed to fail" (p. 5). Woolf's speaker must decide how to use her money justly, and the text painstakingly records her process of deliberation. As they read *Three Guineas* alongside other feminist theory, students ask similar questions: From where does their funding come? How might they spend this cash to make change without reinscribing hierarchical values? What does it mean to advance feminist goals from within institutions that often promote inequity? Despite waves of feminist movements having had rolled by, students quickly realize that today's feminists inherit a world where the problems women face have shifted, but the same violence and patriarchal values that Woolf grapples with persist.

Pointedly, *Three Guineas* calls out higher education, which often reinscribes the very power imbalances its scholars condemn. Woolf's text thus forces students to wrestle with their own privilege and positioning vis-à-vis the communities they serve. The EL project's scaffolded assignments help students to process this moral implication. Initially, students brainstorm ways to spend the grant money, which they now control. By the semester's third week, each student has submitted a grant proposal that identifies a need, describes a plan to address it, and integrates feminist theory. After processing feedback from their peers and the instructor, students discuss all the newly revised proposals, ultimately choosing one. They make their decision based on the criteria they develop in dialogue with course readings. Students then collectively revise the proposal's schedule and budget and take roughly the second half of the semester to implement their plan. While brainstorming, revising, and implementing the project, students individually complete three case studies—in lieu of traditional exams—that evaluate self-selected models of feminist activism. The learning assessment and EL project work together, in this way, to engender an environment of ethical reflection and democratic engagement.

FEMINIST DIALOGUE

Given this admittedly brief background, the co-authors will now assess the project. They have chosen to use dialogue as a means of analysis, because it brings their feminist commitment to counter-normative pedagogy to counter-normative scholarship. Just like hierarchies in the classroom dictate which voices matter, the same hierarchies in scholarship shape which perspectives count as knowledge. Feminist epistemologies therefore insist that, in order to generate useful and liberatory knowledge, scholars need methods that bring them closer to the realities of one another and to the world they share in common (hooks, 1994). By studying WGS 310's project through dialogue, the co-authors recognize that understanding how power works in learning spaces requires educators to start by understanding how power structures their differences and attending to how those differences shape their experience. This recognition includes practices of EL. Thus, while the entirety of this chapter is co-written, we now break to give voice to our different positions. This written correspondence, exchanged during the summer of 2020, attests to feminist EL's ability to raise consciousness of power both inside and outside the classroom.

The Feminist Classroom in the Academy

MM How were you accounting for hierarchy when setting up our class and, given its experiential aspect, in orienting us outside of our classroom?

DJF My approach in the classroom has always been to make those hierarchies part of the conversation. I select course materials that invite critical reflection on power in the academy. This reflection will (hopefully) make the muck and muddle a little less invisible. It also helps students prepare for work in the community. I think many students see higher education—especially in areas like Women's and Gender Studies—as a sort of paradise, a world set apart from oppression, discrimination, and hate. It's a version of the Ivory-Tower fantasy. Of course, we hope to create a little oasis of consciousness-raising and critical reflection, but I do not want to concoct a false paradise.

For this reason, we read *Three Guineas, Teaching to Transgress*, and Adrienne Rich's "Toward a Woman-Centered University" at the outset. How did you experience those texts and discussions as a student? Did they feel relevant to you, or did they come across as me talking shop?

MM I thought that beginning our EL class—a type of class typically aimed at orienting students outside of the classroom—with an emphasis on how power functions inside the classroom was incredibly valuable. This early reflection functioned to break down the false divide between the classroom and the "real" world and help me to consider the feminist classroom as a flawed location within the world rather than just a space from which we learn about the flaws of the world.

As a student with lots of coursework based around social justice, I've witnessed lots of well-intentioned engagement veer dangerously toward a tendency to view education and the accompanying resources as tools to fix the problems of other people. Given that our class had a budget to design a feminist intervention, it was easy to imagine our project falling into a similar pattern. But I think that our reflections on our positions within higher education were valuable in mitigating some of that risk. Lots of our classroom time and approaches to theorizing were focused on learning to listen to one another and care about those experiences. That level of vulnerability was challenging, but it helped us understand that feminist praxis starts with care within our own lives and relationships not in an outside world that needs saving.

What were your goals in designing the class the ways that you did?

DJF In a sense, the entire EL project is an outgrowth of my love of Virginia Woolf—the joy I find in teaching her work—but it also gave me an opportunity to disrupt and redistribute power. Students would ultimately decide how best to move forward, and, in a feminist classroom, that redistribution of power and authority is essential (and not always easy for me, a heavy planner when it comes to teaching!). So, to answer your question, my immediate goals were threefold: (1) redistribute power across the room; (2) trouble the feel-good, quick-fix factor of much service-learning and community engagement, that you address so well above; and (3) allow space for students to create something new and unforeseen. Aware of what you have lovingly termed my fascist tendencies, I funnel most of my planning into applying for the EL grant, preparing the syllabus, and writing the assignments. Then, I (force myself to) take a step back and allow students to learn from each other and the texts.

I intentionally design the EL project to create a learning space where students wrestle with the difficulties of making change in a world whose inequity goes all the way down. That's easier said than done, especially because I have to give up some control. When I think about my fears with regard to EL, they are wildly egocentric. I am always terrified that students will leave the classroom, go out into the world, and embarrass *me* in some way. That fact is not flattering. I should be worried primarily about the harm that they might do to vulnerable populations. But, if I am being honest, that's where the fear starts, and it's not unrelated to worries about my position as junior faculty. It's so much easier to imagine an exam or a paper that stays inside the classroom, where students don't plaster mis-readings of Simone de Beauvoir about town! I know this point seems small, but it's always been the steepest learning curve for me. Whenever students enter into the community, even if it's just the university commu-nity, it is, as a faculty member, difficult; there's a risk there. This project has given me an opportunity to reflect on my own insecurities, but it's a work in progress!

For me, this type of learning is all about the process, so I am wondering what you thought about the process of developing and designing the ini-tiative. After all, that's where my pedagogical goals are grounded: in that process, not in the product.

MM The non-feminist classroom is comfortable because students can rely on their professors for answers and clarity. I'm far more comfortable with the insulated work of identifying injustices than I am with working to remedy them. As a result, I loved Woolf's absolutely formidable style of critique and uncanny ability to shatter her audience's faith in all the insti-tutions they hold dear, but I struggled with learning from feminist theo-ries pointing out all the things people are doing wrong while also trying to discern what we, as a class, could possibly do right.

The premise of EL is, of course, that students learn from their actions and experiences. That's scary for me because learning along the way requires starting without the comfort of answers. Many days my friends and I would leave class in a crisis—certain about nothing except that all our choices inside and outside of the course were implicated in patriarchy.

Without the false certainties academia often offers, this process required a lot of trust: trust that our class could work together, trust that our own intentions were good, trust that we thought through the potential harms, and trust that the world could recover from whatever harms we might have neglected. As our teacher and fearful leader, how could you trust that the good of what we could learn from community engagement would outweigh the potential harm along the way?

DJF It takes an incredible amount of trust, and I am not sure that I could undertake a project of this nature with a large group. There needs to be time and space to digest, to ruminate, and to respond with care. A small class—don't forget that we only had ten in our group—helps, because it allows for individual check-in and consultation. Everyone's voice can be heard and valued in a 75-minute session. Nevertheless, it's always a challenge to cultivate the sort of trust necessary for EL, especially when it comes with a community-engaged component. It's sobering to realize that there is absolutely no way for me to know in advance that the good will outweigh the bad. It's also true that, at UD, we live and learn in an atmosphere of relative privilege. I am potentially allowing students to do harm in a community that is already hard-hit by racial and economic injustices. I take that potential very seriously.

I remind myself, though, that I am a teacher. If we go to school to learn, then how can I possibly expect students to know—at the outset—how to do things just right? My job is to structure a space for learning and to make decisions that support students' ethical movement beyond the classroom. And so, I try to mitigate the potential for harm as much as possible as I scaffold assignments. Hence, my course design made room for copious feedback and multiple revisions. In my comments, I alerted students to potential problems. In some cases, I was blunt, especially if I noticed something that might cause damage. I also trusted you to point out problem areas to each other in class discussion. After all, the goal is to develop habits of critical reflection, and that's ultimately what I am teaching and attempting to model myself.

The Project and the Goals

DJF In designing the class, I hoped to cultivate critical conscientiousness, but this degree of mindfulness is not without drawbacks. You mentioned the anxiety that you experienced, and I remember witnessing it firsthand. I worry that this anxiety will become debilitating, leaving students with a sense that there is *nothing* they can do without causing harm. Would you mind speaking more to that point? I worry sometimes that I create—rather than empowered, critical thinkers—an army of nervous nellies!

MM Feminist consciousness can be as scary as it is useful, and I definitely left your class with the certainty that there's nothing we can do without causing harm (or at least where the potential for harm isn't on the table). I'm not convinced that's a bad place to end up, though.

My anxiety about community engagement has been most debilitating during moments where I've tried to eliminate the potential for harm entirely. In those instances, I figured that if I could understand the different systems of power, then I could pinpoint my position within each system and do something to minimize that risk. This didn't work, and I ended up approaching myself and others as caricatures of our differences and positionality, which left me unable to meet others where they were and recognize their agency. The theory we engaged with, and especially Sara Ahmed, helped me better understand what I was missing.

Ahmed (2017) writes, "There is no guarantee that in struggling for justice we ourselves will be just. We have to hesitate, to temper the strength of our tendencies with doubt, to waver when we are sure, or even because we are sure" (p. 7). The difference here is important—we aren't supposed to wrestle with our doubts until they're gone. We must be humbled enough by those doubts to allow ourselves to be moved.

You mentioned this earlier, but there are no paradises or relationships that exist apart from the violence of the world. That pervasive violence means that harm happens everywhere all the time: our ethical paralysis might stop ourselves from explicit involvement, but it won't stop systems already in motion. While EL raises the stakes by introducing relationships where all sorts of things can go wrong, ultimately our relationships are also the places where good becomes possible. In caring for one another, we learn from another about the world and what we learn equips us to care better.

DJF I learned a lot from Ahmed, too. With her description of care, she reminds us of the pedagogical need to allow for different ideas and unexpected approaches (p. 266). Neither students nor professors should have their answers set in advance of the learning!

On that note, I certainly did not see the initiative that your class developed coming. The project emerged somewhat organically from our discussions as we all became aware of the issue: sexual harassment of student workers. I was not aware of this problem before the class brought my attention to it.

How did the final proposal come together, and how do you feel about the project given that certain elements of it failed to come to fruition?

MM Like you said, our project—a campaign to bring awareness and justice to instances of workplace sexual harassment of students—was shaped by our classmate's experiences as much as it was shaped by the theory that we read. One of our classmates shared that she, along with six of her coworkers, was sexually harassed at their job. When they sought help, their supervisors didn't take their experiences seriously, and the perpetrator kept his job and was hired into the same role.

While we were all horrified by her story, I don't think most of us were surprised. Though no one at UD really speaks about sexual harassment in formal spheres, it's something that gets whispered about everywhere. But when we thought about our experiences through theory, we understood what those experiences reflected about the world we lived in. "Theory," hooks writes, "is not inherently healing, liberatory, or revolutionary. It fulfills this function only when we ask that it do so and direct our theorizing toward this end" (p. 61). Theorizing through our experiences helped us to see the patriarchal violence that allowed sexual harassment to take root, and theorists like Catharine MacKinnon sharpened our understanding of sexual harassment as a tool designed to render women powerless and helped us articulate why we weren't overreacting.

So the project we ended up pitching was designed to bring this discussion into the public sphere. We hired a film student to make a video where students shared their experiences of workplace sexual harassment and planned to launch with a letter-writing campaign. Unfortunately, we ran into some obstacles. Campus was shut down for COVID-19 before we had our event. But our project was also derailed by the same gender-based power issues we tried to address. Because the students in the video depended on their employment to attend UD, we wanted to make sure that they wouldn't lose their jobs for speaking out, so we were careful not to name their employer. And while the video maintained that level of security, the school newspaper was also working on a story about the repeated harassment incidents, and the students in the video were worried about the repercussions of the combined stories. At their request, we're currently holding off on sharing the video and rethinking the best way to share their stories without putting their livelihood or education at risk.

Ahmed talks about diversity work and the "brick walls" that we meet when trying to work for justice within institutions that survive on inequity (p. 142). She shares her own experience speaking up against sexual harassment and the walls that exist for those who want to come forth: students and faculty risk losing their careers, and complaints are silenced so they don't damage the institution. Despite the near impossibility of speaking out, Ahmed reminds us that "Telling the story is part of the feminist battle. A feminist ear can be what we are *for*. The more wearing it is, the more we need to hear" (p. 203). When we let go of the savior complexes that make us feel like we can and must go out into the world and fix what's broken at all costs, we learn new ways to be there and show up for one another.

To Be a Student and a Teacher in Feminist Spaces

MM My major takeaway from this class was that sometimes there's a difference between being a good student and being a good feminist learner. One of the first things we felt when we realized that we weren't going to go forward with our project was guilt. Our class was filled with students who pride themselves on being "good" students, and we were worried that we had failed the project and, in doing so, failed as feminists. You emphasized throughout the semester that we wouldn't be evaluated on how the project went, but it's sometimes hard for students to conceive failure and success outside of the context of formal evaluations. Despite those feelings, I'm proud of our class.

In trusting the people in the video to make the call that they didn't want the video shown, we recognized their stories did not belong to us, and a semester of feminist theory did not give us the authority to decide the purpose they should serve. And even though we did not give the stories the platform that we wanted, I think we still did something important. Our friends were hurt by the sexual harassment that occurred and the failure of those whom they trusted to take them seriously. Through this project, we were able to let our friends know that we heard them, and we were able to offer theory to confirm what they knew about their experiences.

DJF I agree. It seems to me that we often underestimate the power of that feminist ear, but I know, as a teacher, just how powerful listening and acknowledging can be.

I also think we underestimate the power of the feminist err. You mentioned grading earlier, and it's something that I—also one of those "good" students, forever pre-med at heart—take seriously. You'll recall that I graded the assignments surrounding the EL component—reflections and proposals—but I did not grade the end result. I wanted to emphasize the process. In this way, I intentionally made room for failure. And, trust me, it's hard to teach for failure. So much of our pedagogy, especially since No Child Left Behind, is designed to reach objectives, outcomes, and benchmarks. For those of us raised in that environment, it's a challenge to recognize that failure needs to be on the table, that the initiative just might not work. Of course, that doesn't mean we disregard learning outcomes; rather, it means that those outcomes are linked to process rather than product. That approach respects the fact that our action in the world is always messy.

Listening to you reflect on the human and institutional factors that you had to navigate reminds me of why EL is so important for feminist theory. It's one thing to read Ahmed's description of brick walls; it's another thing to run into them. Furthermore, life is full of hap. There will be chance complications, of which COVID-19 is only the most apparent. We need to learn how to learn with and from obstacles, especially since feminist praxis does not end and rarely ends well. It's a way of life. EL in feminist classrooms gives everyone, then, some practice in making social change. An emphasis on that process—on living with failure and against walls—is essential, but there's also a lot of unlearning that needs to happen in this context. Does unlearning seem like the right word to you?

MM I agree with you—if a student's job is learning in order to succeed within the academy, then a feminist student needs to practice that unlearning. As you know, Woolf writes *Three Guineas* at a time when women are being educated, gaining some financial independence, and entering the workforce, and she's worried that once women are absorbed into capitalist and militaristic spaces (such as the university), they'll risk losing their critical eyes.

Woolf, and other thinkers we read in WGS 310, pushed us to balance what we can learn from a space like a classroom with what we lose when we operate from within its walls. Personally, I was most haunted by Woolf's argument that the university has always existed to prepare countries for war, and I kept thinking of what it meant to study justice and peace at a university that received millions of dollars in research funding from the US military. I think one of the biggest questions on all our minds that semester was how could we work for justice from within a space that is—in some important ways—designed for the opposite?

In addition to unlearning, it's also important to consider how we can continue to learn from what Woolf calls "unpaid-for education" (p. 94). For Woolf, women's "unpaid-for education" consists of what women have learned from centuries of being excluded from powerful institutions. These lessons offer strategies for participating within and challenging the makings of power without becoming attached to power's rewards.

At UD, this type of unpaid-for education can be hard to come by. But the right kind of EL, especially when designed to allow for failure, can give us a chance to learn from the gaps of the institutions we so often rely on. I think you're right to emphasize process over product, because those moments where we came up against institutional walls gave us the chance to learn from where certain people and agendas are still excluded from spaces like the university. And most importantly, when we were confronted with instances where our loyalties and priorities as students at a university were in tension with our relationship to our community and our moral convictions, we were empowered and supported in making a choice to be bad students if that meant being just people.

DJF I couldn't have said it better. The danger—for students, staff, and faculty—is to stop asking questions, to assume that our positions within the academy give us special authority or sharper insight, to depreciate knowledge from outside our brick walls. We easily become routinized, "like a gramophone whose needle has stuck" (p. 72), forever circling the mulberry tree. Woolf's speaker puts forward the Society of Outsiders, after all, to strike home the idea that money, status, and power are not enough to change a culture built upon exclusion, violence, and inequality. We need to learn differently. We need not only to study but also to value different subjects. We need to recognize our own implication in the record of injustice and hear anew the differences between me and you.

FEMINIST FAILURE

Feminist EL brings attention to power differentials: between professors and students, between faculty and staff, between university members and community partners. The goal, however, is not to escape the power present in our learning spaces but instead to become increasingly mindful of it. We therefore recommend that EL practitioners employ pedagogical strategies that disturb power dynamics just enough to provoke critical reflection on them. Based on our dialogue, we make three practical suggestions: (1) grade the EL project's process rather than its end product or ultimate success; (2) integrate materials that encourage critical reflection on higher education; and (3) create space for students to share their own expertise, bringing their lives and their interests into the classroom. As critical reflection on relationships becomes part of the curriculum, feminist EL makes possible thoughtful, intentionally disruptive uses of power and new relational configurations. We learn to recognize what we specifically bring as citizens, students, and educators to the table, and, as Woolf's speaker reminds us in *Three Guineas*, "since we are different, our help must be different" (p. 169). We collaborate with attention to those real differences.

Moving forward as feminist learners ultimately means leaving behind the ontological securities wrapped up in the defined roles of teacher and student, along with the positive reinforcement we get when successfully carrying out what those roles ask of us. Even harder: we have to let go of both the notion that service-oriented EL can save a piece of the world and the false promise that the right feminism can save us from moral or political implication. This letting-go is wearying. Rather than resting on easy answers, traditional hierarchies, or elitist epistemologies, feminist pedagogy rests in a restless ambiguity: critical consciousness elevates uncertainty; the urgency of the feminist agenda keeps stakes (and emotions) high; and structural, patriarchal barriers create real and seemingly immovable obstacles. Feminist EL is, therefore, both logistically and emotionally demanding. Our classrooms need to cultivate the sort of trust that shares power and authority, in part, because emotional support of each other is necessary. The brick walls of academia falsely protect some from the daily muddle of a world where patriarchy runs deep and justice is unlikely, but feminist EL brings us forward toward complex relationships where love not only makes failing at justice scary but also lays the groundwork for a space where change becomes possible together.

Acknowledgments This chapter builds on conversations with the following members of WGS 310: Sarah Critchfield, Kaycee Curtis, Olivia Hendershott, Elyse McMahon, Fiona O'Malley, Yulianna Otero, Tess Poe-Slade, and Ruthey Schultz.

REFERENCES

Ahmed, S. (2017). *Living a feminist life*. Duke University Press.

Clayton, P., Hess, G., Hartman, E., Edwards, K. E., Shackford-Bradley, J., Harrison, B., & McLaughlin, K. (2014). Educating for democracy by walking the talk in experiential learning. *Journal of Applied Learning in Higher Education, 6*, 3–35.

hooks, b. (1994). *Teaching to transgress: Education as the practice of freedom*. Routledge.

Kolb, D. A. (1984). *Experiential learning: Experience as the source of learning and development*. Prentice-Hall.

Meagher, S. M. (2015). Feminist philosophy and civic engagement. In J. Oxley & R. Ilea (Eds.), *Experiential learning in philosophy* (1st ed., pp. 149–157). Routledge.

Oxley, J., & Ilea, R. (2015). Experiential learning in philosophy: Theory and practice. In J. Oxley & R. Ilea (Eds.), *Experiential learning in philosophy* (1st ed., pp. 1–18). Routledge.

Saltmarsh, J., Hartley, M., & Clayton, P. (2009). Democratic engagement white paper. *New England resource center for higher education*. http://repository. upenn.edu/gse_pubs/274

Woolf, V. (1938). *Three guineas* (2006 annotated ed.). Harcourt.

CHAPTER 10

Learning from Faith-Based Cross-Cultural Immersions

Nick Cardilino, Samantha Kennedy, and Mary Niebler

"Now I get what the Paschal Mystery is," the student said. The group had just left the Chapel at the University of Central America in San Salvador after looking at actual photos of the crime scene from the slaughter of six Jesuit theologians, their housekeeper, and their daughter. In place of traditional Stations of the Cross on the walls, the Chapel had sketches drawn from actual photographs of people tortured during the War. This was one of the final stops after a week of visiting important places and talking to ordinary people to learn about the Salvadoran Civil War and the current economic, social, political, and religious issues faced by the people. The University of Dayton delegation was just outside the Chapel in silence for a few minutes, not because the leaders had asked everyone to do that; it just felt right and necessary for the individuals to be in private reflection. There had been group reflections each day on the day's experiences, but the Catholic tenet of the Paschal Mystery had never come up in

N. Cardilino (✉) • S. Kennedy • M. Niebler
Center for Social Concern, University of Dayton, Dayton, OH, USA
e-mail: ncardilino1@udayton.edu; skennedy2@udayton.edu;
mniebler1@udayton.edu

discussion. So, after breaking the silence and making this statement unprompted, the student had to explain what she was talking about. She said she had experienced the Good Friday suffering and death throughout the week in all that she saw and heard, but had also managed to find the hope of Easter resurrection in the people and in this recently built Chapel.

This story exemplifies the co-curricular EL programs coordinated by the Center for Social Concern (CSC). This Center is a part of Campus Ministry at the University of Dayton, a Catholic and Marianist institution. The CSC provides students with a wide array of opportunities to put "faith into action for social justice and peace. [That] action... includes prayer, advocacy for positive change, service, critical reflection, equitable relationship-building, raising awareness of social and environmental justice issues, and leadership formation" (University of Dayton Center for Social Concern, n.d.). The CSC's primary learning objective, then, is for students to deepen their spirituality and faith life by becoming aware of and taking action for the common good. This learning objective is and our programs are for all students regardless of religious tradition, major, socio-economic background, or any other demographic difference.

Although the CSC holds discussions on social justice issues as they relate to faith, speakers, panel presentations, films, and so on, students tell us that the most significant faith development happens in EL opportunities. We organize faith-based cross-cultural immersion trips to help students attain our main learning objective in the following experiential ways: (1) encountering cultures and approaches to life that are different from their own (2) witnessing examples of economic inequality, social and political injustice, and environmental concerns that most of our students haven't seen before, (3) watching and listening to local community leaders who are working for change and, of course, (4) reflecting on those encounters. After a rationale for our learning objective and a description of the immersion experiences that we organize each year, this chapter will show how these four methods enable students to grow in their faith life by becoming aware of and taking action for the common good.

Development Beyond Cognitive

Through our immersive programs, students gain some significant cognitive content, particularly Catholic social teaching principles (solidarity, human dignity, care for God's creation, etc.) and social justice teachings within their own faith traditions whatever those traditions may be. We also provide content on leadership, particularly for those students who take on the role of a leader in one of these programs. In addition, participants learn about the specific location of the trip—its population, culture, history, religion, and the economic and social justice issues it faces.

However, our work and our primary learning objective bring many of the more nebulous elements of the University of Dayton's Mission and Identity to life, especially educating the whole person, linking learning and scholarship with leadership and service, and critically evaluating our times (University of Dayton, n.d.).

Our primary learning objective is not cognitive development; it is faith development. Plus, a significant part of faith development is moral development. James Fowler (faith development), Lawrence Kohlberg, Carol Gilligan, and Jonathan Haidt (moral development) are some of the most significant thinkers on these topics over the past 40 years and have influenced our work.

The moral development part of our learning objective is a social ethics perspective rooted in the Catholic Church's social teaching, articulated well in the World Synod of Catholic Bishops' document *Justicia in Mundo* (1971): "Action on behalf of justice and participation in the transformation of the world fully appear to us as a constitutive dimension of the preaching of the Gospel, or, in other words, of the Church's mission for the redemption of the human race and its liberation from every oppressive situation" (para. 6).

Even if we weren't part of Campus Ministry at a Catholic University, Strain (2005) provides five reasons why it is appropriate for all higher education institutions to be in the business of formation of moral character:

> First, all education, to the degree that it has any impact, is character forming. Even the most value-neutral course conveys the value of rational inquiry as a guiding principle in human life. Second, if we as educators are always implicitly affecting students' moral development across its four components, we ought to become conscious explicitly of how we are doing so. Third, the liberal arts, as I understand them, are in the business of liberating the potential of students to actualize the good as well as the true and the beautiful. Fourth, openness to a plurality of visions of the good and enabling students to examine alternative visions critically are key to this liberation. Fifth, service-learning courses do not, in fact, lead to uniform visions of the good or to a linear moral development. (pp. 69–70)

Moral development is necessary for both citizenship and discipleship. Public higher education institutions in the US were founded in large part to educate people for citizenship. Faith-based institutions were founded to educate people of faith for Christian (usually) discipleship. There are some differences between the two, but citizenship and discipleship share much in common. After describing some of the significant tensions between them in "The Two Pedagogies: Discipleship and Citizenship," John A. Coleman (1988) argues that "the Church that educates for discipleship must also concern itself with education for citizenship" (p. 36). Two similarities between these two that require the development of character are taking action for the common good and creating a more just society. Kolb's (1984) four modes of EL, especially "reflective observation" and "abstract conceptualization," are key to both citizenship and discipleship. We in the Center for Social Concern weave both into the opportunities we provide students. It's no wonder that students of all faiths as well as atheists and agnostics are not only invited to participate, but do so. Thus, while faith development remains our main focus, the development of active citizens of good character is a secondary goal.

Eyler and Giles (1999), Colby, Ehrlich, Beaumont, and Stephens (2003), Strain (2005), Schutte, and Wetmore (2012), and others provide strong evidence that experiential education, particularly service-learning and civic engagement, affects moral development in profound ways:

> As individuals move through the successive stages [of moral development], their moral judgment moves from simple conceptions of morality grounded in unilateral authority and individual reciprocity to judgments grounded in shared social norms to an appreciation of a more complex social system to a perspective that is capable of evaluating the existing social system in relation to more fundamental principles of justice. (Colby et al., 2003, pp. 103–104)

A specific moral development that is taught by the Catholic Church as essential to faith is a movement from a charity-only stage to one that takes action for social justice in addition to charity. Pope Pius XI spelled out the moral development of this Christian requirement: "Charity will never be true charity unless it takes justice into account.... Let no one attempt with small gifts of charity to exempt themselves from the great duties imposed by justice" (*Divini Redemptorus*, 1937). After every hands-on charitable service we offer, we are sure to ask questions of participants about the social justice implications of what they have experienced and how changes in laws, policies, and systems might alleviate the need for that charity.

IMMERSION PROGRAMS

In addition to many EL opportunities such as one day of service experiences and service clubs, the CSC offers longer programs through domestic and international immersions. These include a local program called REAL Dayton, alternative break trips—both domestic and international—that we call BreakOut trips, Summer Cross-Cultural Immersion trips, and the UD Summer Appalachia Program. In his latest encyclical, *Fratelli Tutti*, Pope Francis (2020) reiterates St. Francis of Assisi's call for a "love that transcends the barriers of geography and distance…. St. Francis expressed the essence of a fraternal openness that allows us to acknowledge, appreciate and love each person, regardless of physical proximity, regardless of where he or she was born or lives" (para. 1). Yet, he also discusses the importance of learning this "fraternity and social friendship" locally within the context of one's family. Having both local and distance programs allows students to expand their notions of solidarity (Table 10.1).

REAL Dayton is a local community engagement immersion. REAL is an acronym that stands for Reach out, Encounter Dayton, Act with others, and Lead together. The "Reach Out" aspect gets students off campus, out of their comfort zone, and open to learning something new. "Encounter Dayton" pushes students to engage with the city and its people, while recognizing the gifts of the city and the passionate citizens who make Dayton the special place it is. Some of these gifts include a growing downtown, being a welcoming and immigrant-friendly community, expansive arts offerings, and the natural environment, fed by the confluence of five rivers. Participants "Act with Others" as they serve in collaboration with local partners working to address the challenges Dayton faces, such as segregation, disinvestment, the opioid epidemic, and food insecurity. Finally, "Lead Together" means leading collaboratively with Daytonians and fellow UD students to build a stronger community moving toward the common good. Prayer and reflection are interspersed throughout the four-day experience, to meet the CSC's primary learning objective. The 2–3 student directors and 14–16 other student leaders take a mini-course on leadership for the common good, faith in action, community engagement, and the practical design of the REAL Dayton experience. Mini-courses are short-term classes that are offered free for enrolled

Table 10.1 Programs from the past few years

Program	Location(s)	Time of year	Length	Number of students
REAL Dayton	Dayton, OH	Fall break (early October)	4 days	50–75
Fall BreakOuts	Salyersville, KY St. Louis, MO	Fall break (early October)	4 days	16–20
Winter BreakOuts	Tijuana, Mexico Belize City, Belize San Salvador, El Salvador E. St. Louis, IL Nazareth Farm, WV Houston, TX	Winter break (early January)	10 days	36–48
Spring BreakOuts	Quito, Ecuador San Juan, PR Salyersville, KY Chicago, IL St. Louis, MO Wall Twp., NJ	Spring break (mid-March)	10 days	40–60
May BreakOuts	Memphis, TN/ Birmingham, AL/ Montgomery, AL/Atlanta, GA (Civil Rights Tour) Los Angeles, CA New Orleans, LA	Week after commencement (early to mid-May)	10 days	10–20
Summer Cross-cultural Immersion trips	Quetzaltenango, Guatemala Ranchi and Bangalore, India Lubwe, Zambia Kumba, Cameroon	Summer break	4–8 weeks	16–32
UD Summer Appalachia Program	Salyersville, KY	Summer break	9 weeks	12–14

students and are often only one credit. This format for the student leaders fosters commitment and educational structure without overburdening their schedules or credit load.

We offer students two basic types of BreakOuts (alternative break trips), although there is often overlap on each trip. The first type is those focused on charitable hands-on service to a community in need, especially in disaster relief situations, such as in New Orleans or the New Jersey coast. Others, such as those in El Salvador or Los Angeles, allow students to learn about social justice issues through encounters with community members, listening to their stories of joy and struggle in an unequal world. All of our BreakOuts employ reflection and prayer to meet our learning goal and deepen what is gained through personal experience and relationship-building. Schutte and Wetmore offer an important critique of these trips: "...sustainable change requires much more than one trip or a few weeks out of their life. They need to be part of the solution by 'what they purchase', 'how they vote', 'what they read', 'what they advocate for' and various other behaviors" (2012). We work intentionally with our location-based partners and in our orientations and post-trip reflections to drive this message home in the hope that the experience will motivate these life-long effects.

Our Summer Cross-cultural Immersion trips provide students with a longer, more in-depth experience of community-based global learning. Summer immersions are four- to eight-week-long journeys with our partners in countries such as Guatemala, India, Cameroon, and Zambia. Through a spring semester mini-course, travelers prepare together for their summer experience. These experiences are generally non-credit bearing, although students do receive one credit hour for the preparation mini-course. Those traveling to Guatemala can earn up to 12 credit hours in Spanish. Some students have used their experiences in these locations to conduct independent studies for credit.

What began as a purely charity-focused program initiated by students in 1965 evolved into the UD Summer Appalachia Program (UDSAP) by the early 1990s, a much more intentionally relational program with the people of Salyersville, KY, in Magoffin County, one of the economically poorest counties in Appalachia. The work now performed by the students—running a day camp for young children, a teen center, and visiting people in the nursing home—makes UDSAP more relational, educational, and immersive than the previous work of delivering donated goods and doing home repairs.

This change to UDSAP, as well as our approach in the design of REAL Dayton, BreakOuts, and Cross-cultural Immersions, has been strongly influenced by Paolo Friere. Friere (1970) calls for "radical conscientization," that is, starting the EL process by listening to people on the margins. "One cannot expect positive results from an educational or political action program which fails to respect the particular view of the world held by the people. Such a program constitutes cultural invasion, good intentions notwithstanding" (p. 95). In the EL programs described in this chapter, our intention is always to begin with listening to the needs and desires of the people we meet and allowing them to drive the agenda, rather than imposing white American cultural ideas. Any "service" that is done in these experiences only happens when it is requested by those Friere would call the "oppressed." A quote students often use in their journals and final reflection papers, attributed to Lilla Watson, says. "If you have come here to help me, you are wasting your time. But if you have come because your liberation is bound up with mine, then let us work together."

In the UDSAP program, for example, the people of Salyersville considered their own needs and have asked students in the program to create and run a fun and educational day camp for elementary school children and an evening program for teens. They are also pleased that the group visits the local nursing home a couple of times a week. In this mutual exchange, the community members give back to the students by teaching them about Appalachian culture, faith practices, and family values. In fact, many families invite the UD students into their homes and their lives. Pope Francis speaks often about these mutually beneficial cross-cultural relationships that begin with dialogue by using the word *encuentro,* or encounter. We will explore some examples of *encuentro* students have experienced in the next section.

ENCOUNTERING DIFFERENT CULTURES AND APPROACHES TO LIFE

Our great challenge is to create a culture of encounter which encourages individuals and groups to share the richness of their traditions and experience; to break down walls and to build bridges. The Church in America as elsewhere is called to go out from its comfort zone and be a leaven of communion; communion among ourselves, with our fellow Christians, and with all who seek a future of hope. (Francis, 2016)

Creating a "culture of encounter" leads to solidarity. One student explored the sense of solidarity she felt through sharing a faith experience while on immersion in Guatemala in 2019:

Seeing families together moved me to tears. I was so inspired by this beautiful faith and I missed home so much in that moment. Faithfulness and spirituality are a whole other ballpark outside of the United States, and there is so much I can learn from other cultures. This is something that is really important to me not only as a person, but as someone who is studying to become a religion teacher.

Recognizing the intersection of culture, faith, and national identity may push this student to be a more aware and well-rounded teacher of religion upon graduation.

In recent years, we have adopted the concept of "global service learning" or "community-based global learning" which actually expresses better what our programs have been doing for a long time even though we just called it "service learning." Whitehead (2015) differentiates between SL and global SL by saying that global SL

> requires deep, grounded knowledge of community cultures along with respect for the knowledge and experiences of community members. Attention to cultural, economic, historical, political, and social issues affecting the community, as well as to those issues' local and international contexts, is essential (Longo and Saltmarsh 2011). Global service learning affords students opportunities to understand the larger structural forces underlying social problems, provides transformational learning experiences, and helps students see the world in a profoundly different way. (Kiely, 2004)

For students to enter into a Global SL cross-cultural encounter, we aim to provide them with the proper resources in their preparation. Our longer immersion experiences require weekly meetings or a mini-course prior to travel, which takes students through an exploration of understanding their own cultural identities, as well as researching and sharing the cultural customs or their host community. Most importantly, students are asked to recognize and explore the complexities and power dynamics that may exist when a group of students from a private US university is welcomed by a community different from themselves.

Occasionally, these dynamics can play out among group members, who through the deeper exploration of their own personal and cultural identities may find some similarities and differences, which leads to greater learning and understanding. As students learn more about themselves, their group members, and their host communities, we encourage reflective journaling to enhance that learning process.

Global SL isn't only appropriate when entering a culture in a foreign country. In the US, the Appalachian culture is quite different from the American culture most of our students grew up in. One UDSAPer describes his Global SL experience as one of growth that is caused by witnessing a different way of life for nine weeks: "In the beginning you think you are helping them by providing an outlet, but in reality it is them who are helping you grow. Grow in ways that only you will understand. I got way more out of my summer than any of the people got out of me."

Among our more specific list of Global SL objectives for UDSAP are for students to understand the Appalachian culture more deeply and to understand themselves. Here's part of a poem in which one student spelled out some things that she learned about the Appalachian people and herself:

> I learned to listen.
> I learned to listen to the "grumpy old woman" who frowned more than she breathed.
> I learned to listen to the woman who screamed and yelled out obscenities; who cried out of loneliness.
> I learned to listen to the man who reprimanded us for not playing BINGO right.
> I learned to listen to the sweet woman who welcomed all with a smile and a prayer, and who owned the gift of hospitality like it was her kidney.
> I listened, and I heard their call to be loved, and their call to be seen for more than they appeared.
> As I got better at listening, I saw their smiles of being heard, and being love.

Through EL, this student developed and fine-tuned her listening skills to come to greater understanding of not only cross-cultural exchange and growth, but also the human experience through true connection.

Sometimes, "encuentro" can cause culture shock. One UDSAP participant recalled an orientation session about the culture shock they would likely experience: "Little did I know then, but that culture shock would take a huge turn nine weeks later, as I returned to mainstream America, walking back onto UD's campus, and feeling an overwhelming sense of emptiness." He then talked about how the cultural differences he learned about through experience led to his reverse culture shock. "As all UDSAPers know, there's something so indescribably special and unique about that summer in Appalachia, one that can never fully be matched by other experiences. The peace and tranquility I felt there, the sense of home and belonging, and the feeling of reciprocal love can truly overpower you."

Witnessing Economic Inequality, Social and Political Injustice, and Environmental Concerns

During REAL Dayton, students participate in three service projects with their small groups. Two service projects are done in partnership with a local nonprofit organization and the third experience is done in a local neighborhood. Each of the service experiences has an element of orientation, education about the organization or neighborhood, and then action. Whether their service projects are doing laundry at a local homeless shelter, sorting and cleaning items at the Food Bank, doing awareness raising activities about domestic violence with the YWCA, or working at an urban farm on abandoned lots in a low-income neighborhood, REAL Dayton participants are witnessing what many haven't seen before and responding to Pope Francis' spiritual challenge: "…The Church in the United States [must] respond to the challenge of going beyond what is comfortable, business as usual, to become a leaven of communion for all those who seek a future of hope, especially young people and families that live in the peripheries of society" (Francis, 2016).

There are many different types of injustices students witness on BreakOuts, Immersions, and UDSAP as well. Like REAL Dayton, all of these trips provide some powerful views of poverty—mostly urban, Appalachian, or global poverty. "Investing an entire summer to live and understand the struggle of poverty only scratches the surface," said one UDSAPer. Racial injustice is seen on many of these experiences, especially the Civil Rights Tour, in which the group travels to Memphis, Birmingham, Montgomery, and Atlanta to learn from residents, museums, and simply being in the places that were important to the history of the civil rights movement. Trips to Belize and Tijuana not only expose deep poverty but also inequalities in education. The L'Arche community in St. Louis teaches students a great deal about the social justice issues experienced by people with disabilities. Environmental justice issues are clear in trips to Houston and Ecuador.

In Ecuador, the group tours the Otonga Reserve in the Otonga Cloud forest. From the tour guide, students learn of the biological significance of the region, the indigenous peoples who rely on the forest, and some of the modern dangers facing the forest and its people. Students take time to reflect on the themes of global solidarity and care and stewardship for God's creation. One participant said,

I could probably write a book on everything that I learned from this experience. Being an environmental biology major, this trip really taught me how much I waste during the week. Also, it really taught me how disconnected we are from the environment in the US and how much we disrespect nature. In Ecuador they grow up in nature, respecting it and using it to its full extent. Furthermore, some of the people that we worked with were scientists and it really made me excited about my major because they were so passionate about their work.... This trip really makes me want to give back to the community more because this was the best ten days of my life.

In EL programs where students are able to witness the struggles of injustice and inequality, and notice their own life's disconnections to humanity, or in this case, the natural world, the lines between "us and them" become less clear. This learning comes from listening to the experience of the community members they encounter.

WATCHING AND LISTENING TO LOCAL COMMUNITY LEADERS

While all of our cross-cultural immersion experiences contain an element of learning from community leaders about how they work for change, this is very much at the forefront of REAL Dayton, BreakOut trips to El Salvador and Los Angeles, and the summer immersion in India.

There are a variety of components of REAL Dayton that give students exposure to local community leaders:

- A bus and walking tour of Dayton which includes a stop at City Hall where we talk to one of the City Commissioners.
- A panel of local leaders who share the work they are doing in the city and have time to dialogue with the students.
- We also have speakers from local organizations during our lunchtimes.
- Leaders at the various service sites begin each project with an orientation and often spend time talking with the students as they do their hands-on work.
- Participants eat one dinner in the house of a Dayton citizen(s) and leader(s) with their small group.

REAL Dayton student leaders not only get content on leadership theories and skills from the mini-course, but their understanding is multiplied by their interactions with these community leaders with whom we interact.

In their final reflection papers and exit interviews, they often reflect on their understanding of how to lead and their increased commitment to staying civically engaged post-REAL Dayton. One wrote: "It was valuable for me to meet all of the community members and leaders. I heard so many unique stories and experiences. It's crazy to think we all live within a few miles of each other, and we all come from different backgrounds. REAL Dayton has encouraged me to stay active in my community and meet more people from all different walks of life." There is a statistically significant increase from pre- to post-survey answers in the participants' agreement with the statement "I feel like there are people in the Dayton community actively working to address the city's challenges." Many participants do decide to stay and live in the city of Dayton after graduation. Those who live elsewhere discuss how their REAL Dayton experience has impacted them to get involved wherever they are living post-graduation.

Similar to REAL Dayton, the EL Salvador BreakOut primarily relies on interacting with community leaders. They share personal experiences of the Salvadoran Civil War, the roles they played out of their sense of religious and civic duty, and the influence of Archbishop (now Saint) Oscar Romero on their leadership. However, their examples don't stop in the 1970s; they also discuss what is happening today socially, politically, and religiously. They talk about the negative impact of "Free Trade Zones" and sweatshops. Basically, they talk about how they are leading for justice today.

Students on the Los Angeles BreakOut often find the most significant part of the trip in spending time listening, watching, and interacting with Fr. Greg Boyle, SJ. He is the bestselling author, speaker, and founder of Homeboy Industries, a very successful program aimed at getting gang members into decent jobs. His story of learning about the neighborhood when he was assigned there and how he eventually became a leader for social change is very inspiring to our students—even more so as they hear from the former gang members there and see the place where it all happens.

Our Summer Cross-cultural Immersion trip to India is yet another example of students learning from community leaders. They spend two weeks in Ranchi and three weeks in Bangalore with the Marianist brothers and sisters (the same religious group that founded the University of Dayton). They run a program called REDS which feeds, provides health care, and educates children from the slums. The older children are taught skilled trades so that they don't have to return to looking through garbage for recyclables to earn a few pennies. In Kolkata, they visit Mother Teresa's Home for the Dying and Destitute, which is still run by the religious order she founded, the Missionaries of Charity. The Marianist brothers and sisters and the Charity sisters provide great examples in word and deed for our students about what it means to be a community leader, providing students with much to process and reflect upon.

REFLECTING ON THE EXPERIENCES

In *Community-Based Global Learning: The Theory and Practice of Ethical Engagement at Home and Abroad*, Hartman, Kiely, Boettcher, and Friedrichs (2018) point to the importance of critical reflection during an EL event or program and how "reflective tools can support CBGL participants' personal, spiritual, political, social, emotional, intercultural, moral, and academic development during programs" (Hartman et al., p. 60). We would add that all of the world's most respected spiritual leaders throughout history agree that prayerful or meditative reflection is essential to spiritual growth. Students need time to process and reflect upon their own values and to see what drives them to live out a commitment to active citizenship and leadership for the common good.

In a typical year when students will be traveling for four to six weeks in the summer, we begin meeting in February. Students are first asked to begin a self-reflection process, identifying their own cultural identities and how that may influence how they related to the world around them. In *Beyond Guilt Trips: Mindful Travel in an Unequal World*, Dr. Anu Taranath (2019) takes an in-depth dive into the accountability and impacts we must attend to with community-based learning around the globe. Through storytelling and listening, Taranath asserts that "to approach our travel opportunities with critical awareness and reflection, we'll have to slow down our revved up desire to go and instead, first consider some big issues" (30). These issues especially include how a traveler or experiential learner's own identity might play a role in their experience and relationship across differences. Without an understanding of how and why the world is so unequal, we may never achieve a more equal human experience across the globe.

So, in all of the EL immersion programs we run, we are sure to include opportunities and prompting questions for reflection to occur. The methods we use include journal writing (often with prompts), small group and large group discussion, creative group activities, prayer, evaluation forms, final reflection papers and presentations, exit interviews, even art projects. The questions we ask flow from the "What, So What, Now What?" model (Rolfe et al., 2001). This model is an approachable way to allow students to begin to dive deeper into some of the pressing structural injustices students face in community-based learning, as well as getting them thinking on action steps. This model is also adaptable and a simple go-to tool for group leaders who can't come up with a good question on the spot.

The UDSAP program begins with a semester-long orientation that covers a wide variety of topics from deciding which students will take on which tasks to an overview of Appalachian culture from experts. In the students' nine-week-long experience, in addition to many informal reflections each day, they hold slightly more structured weekly group reflection sessions that usually take over three hours. They are also strongly encouraged to do individual reflection through journaling. Some also use art and even video production (with great sensitivity to the people of the Salyersville community) as part of their individual reflections.

Evaluations after BreakOuts reveal the importance of nightly reflection. On the March 2019 Ecuador BreakOut, three students observed: "The reflection process really helped me put words to what I was feeling during this trip: the joy of the community I felt among the others who went on this trip. It was a reflection full of emotion," and "the reflection process was awesome because it tied together spirituality with the trip and allowed us some time to think about the magnitude of what we did each day." Finally, "It helped me be more grateful of myself and the people on the trip. I truly felt like I was growing each night, as if I was taking in everything during the trip, as well as making me think about how I can apply the experiences back home and at UD." The students go on to share where they find value in the EL process, "The most valuable part of the experience was being able to learn from the culture by talking with the locals (I had the advantage of being a Spanish-speaker) Therefore, I truly appreciate that I was able to talk with the driver, the agronomer on the trip, and the tour guide," and "the most valuable part of this experience was talking to and living with people of a different culture, practicing my Spanish, and growing in my understanding of conservation efforts across the globe."

This example highlights how even a ten-day experience, coupled with intentional guided reflection, can push students to grow spirituality and in community, and gain a wider lens in which to analyze and understand the world around them. We have found through post-BreakOut evaluations that a great majority of students who attend any BreakOut experience, whether domestic or international, for four days or ten days, agree or strongly agree that the experience has "encouraged (them) to respond to the call of the Gospel to make service a part of (their) life." (Post-BreakOut reflections, cumulative, 2015–2019.) This encouragement is and the desire to continue to serve is the fruit of an experience of learning that goes beyond the cerebral.

In a reflection on his UDSAP experience, one participant encapsulated our primary learning objective about growing in faith by participating in awareness of and action for social and environmental justice when he wrote,

> When I first arrived I thought God was more present here--in these hills, in this house and especially in these people; but over time I realized that the change was in me, not God. I was more present to God. I was following His command of Love. Through the good, the bad and the painful, Love was always a visible constant.

In addition to spiritual growth, we often see other aspects of their personal development in students' reflections. Sometimes their immersion experiences impact their chosen career. Here, a member of the 2019 India Immersion reflects, "Overall, my experience in India is one I will keep with me for the rest of my life. As I look forward to my career in music therapy, I am reminded of the weight of cultural barriers/differences and how they affect how to form relationships with others."

Sometimes, the personal growth that comes from reflection is too multi-faceted to fit into a single theme, such as this one from an international student from China after her BreakOut trip to New Orleans: "it (reflection) help(ed) me cultivate a positive attitude to face my life, overcome difficulties I met and to meet and improve myself in the future. I learned how to work well with patience and heart and how to cooperate with other people to finish work as a team group. I learned how to jump over culture differences and diversity to communicate with natives and make friends with them. I improved my oral English skill and obtained a deep insight into local people and culture."

Despite these examples of spiritual and personal development, the reflection that happens in these immersions often bleeds into cognitive learning about social problems, especially what faith traditions have to say about them. Since our immersions are conducted within the framework of Catholic Social Teaching, participants become able to name and define the themes of CST and to witness them coming to life. These themes come from church documents on social justice issues and include the dignity of the human person, the common good and community, a preferential option for the poor, rights and responsibilities, the role of government and subsidiarity, economic justice, stewardship of God's creation, a pro-motion of peace and disarmament, participation in society, global solidar-ity and development, and a care for God's creation. CST is usually introduced to all travelers in the pre-departure preparation to help stu-dents to frame their experience within a faith or set of values.

In the REAL Dayton mini-course, for example, the leaders dive deeply into CST and learn to connect faith and action so they can model that and assist participants in their own reflections. In a final reflection paper, one student leader in a final reflection paper shared:

> From discussion in class, it made me realize even more how faith and social justice and action can be connected. I am already passionate about social justice, but adding a deeper meaning by connecting faith adds another dimension of passion. Before this mini-course I guess it never really clicked in me that I could connect these in my own life, having the knowledge of the Catholic Social Teaching principles and having a passion for social jus-tice. In my own life and future, I hope to continue to hold these principles close to me.

In the past two years, when Summer Cross-cultural Immersion stu-dents are asked to set learning goals for their experience, we have asked them to identify at least one theme of Catholic Social Teaching along with one of the UN Sustainable Development Goals as a way to frame their learning. The connections students begin to make pre-departure, while reflecting during the experience, and upon re-entry to their home envi-ronment have proven to show growth in learning and a hopeful promise for continued work for change.

The reflections from students and connections made through their immersion experiences abroad are full of challenging questions, moments of identity crises, guilt of privilege, and wonders of their place in the world.

The great importance of these questions and reflections has us always looking to improve the process for the students.

Conclusion

While we are proud of the work we do in planning these trips and developing tools for reflection, we know that we have much to learn, and there are a number of challenges we face.

As we write, our major challenge has been the suspension of all of our trips due to COVID-19 restraints on travel. We are working to continue our connections with our partners around the world, and connect students to meaningful virtual experiences across cultures in the interim. The students who were chosen for the UDSAP program for summer 2020 were not only disappointed to have their summer experience canceled, but being in the middle of orientation, they had a strong desire to continue to learn about Appalachian culture. So, they did. They kept their weekly meeting time and took turns doing some research and sharing it with the others in the group. In fall 2020, REAL Dayton went on with the leader mini-course; those leaders created an alternative, mostly virtual program in which Dayton community leaders came to speak to the group via Zoom and community partners made videos of their organizations and the volunteer work the students would have done. There was still plenty of time for small group discussions. Evaluations were very positive and the normal number of students participated. Even two of the BreakOut trips are continuing without travel—El Salvador and Nazareth Farm, WV. Our partners in both of those locations have developed alternative virtual cultural learning programs that will have speakers, videos of the locations they would have gone to, and so on. Both are scheduled for spring semester 2021.

A second challenge we face on a regular basis is finding group leaders. All of our Summer Cross-cultural Immersions, international BreakOuts, some domestic BreakOuts, and UDSAP require faculty or staff leaders. We sometimes make exceptions to allow graduate students to lead them, but the challenge remains because of the required time commitment. We have been able to offer small stipends to those leading summer programs, but it remains difficult to recruit them.

Like faculty and staff, it should be noted that not all students are able to take four–eight weeks of their summer away from work or family to travel. Although we offer a robust scholarship program for these cross-cultural immersions, students may find the time and financial burden a barrier to participation.

Another challenge we are currently addressing is that while we have student evaluations for all of these programs, those evaluation tools are inconsistent with each other. This makes it difficult to incorporate data for a broader view of these programs as a whole.

While there are many good examples of students achieving our main personal faith and spirituality objective, we continue to look for ways to strengthen these examples. This task is made more difficult, however, with each generation. A Barna Group study released in 2018 "indicates that 35 percent of Generation Z teens considered themselves to be atheist, agnostic or not affiliated with any religion. By comparison, only 30 percent of millenials, 30 percent of Generation X and 26 percent of Baby Boomers said the same" (Smith, 2018). Nevertheless, the challenge is necessary to take on the mission of our Center, of the University, and of the Church.

Taranath (2019) ends her *Beyond Guilt Trips* with the quip, "If the unexamined life is not worth living, the unexamined trip might not be worth taking" (Taranath, p. 229). Let us hope continued examination proves the experiences worth it.

REFERENCES

Colby, A., Ehrlich, T., Beaumont, E., & Stephens, J. (2003). *Educating citizens: Preparing American undergraduates for lives of moral and civic responsibility.* Jossey-Bass.

Coleman, SJ. J. A. (1988). "The two pedagogies: Discipleship and citizenship" in Education for citizenship and discipleship, edited by Mary C. Boys. : Pilgrim Press, 35–75.

Eyler, J., & Giles, D. E. (1999). *Where's the Learning in Service-Learning.* Jossey-Bass.

Francis, P. (2016). *Video message for V Encuentro.* https://vencuentro.org/pope-francis-message-for-the-v-encuentro/

Francis, P. (2020). *Fratelli tutti.* http://www.vatican.va/content/francesco/en/encyclicals/documents/papa-francesco_20201003_enciclica-fratelli-tutti.html

Friere, P. (1970). *Pedagogy of the oppressed.* Continuum.

Hannibal, L. C. (2020). *Reaching out, encountering Dayton, acting with others, leading together: Assessing college student experiences in a community engagement program* (Unpublished senior project capstone). University of Dayton.

Hartman, E., Kiely, R., Boettcher, C., & Friedrichs, J. (2018). *Community-based global learning: The theory and practice of ethical engagement at home and abroad.* Stylus.

Kiely, R. (2004) . A Chameleon with a Complex: Searching for Transformation in International Service-learning. *Michigan Journal of Community Service Learning, 10*(2), 5–20.

Kolb, D. A. (1984). *Experiential learning: Experience as the source of learning and development.* Prentice-Hall.

Longo, N. V, & Saltmarsh, J. (2011). *New Lines of Inquiry in Reframing International Service Learning Into Global Service Learning.* Stylus Publishing, LLC.

Pius XI, P. (1937). *Divini redemptorus.* http://www.vatican.va/content/pius-xi/en/encyclicals/documents/hf_p-xi_enc_19370319_divini-redemptoris.html

Rolfe, G., Freshwater, D., & Jasper, M. (2001). *Critical reflection in nursing and the helping professions: A user's guide.* Palgrave Macmillan.

Schutte, K. J., & Wetmore, L. (2012). Experiential learning as a catalyst for moral development in cognitive growth. *International Journal of Business and Social Science, 3*(19).

Smith, S. (2018). Gen Z is the Least Christian Generation in American History, Barna Finds. *Christian Post.* Retrieved from https://www.christianpost.com/news/gen-z-is-the-least-christian-generation-in-american-history-barna-finds.html

Strain, C. R. (2005). Pedagogy and practice: Service learning and students' moral development. In Laff, N. S. (ed.) *New directions for teaching and learning* (Vol. 2005, Issue 103 Special Issue: Identity, learning, and the liberal arts Autumn (Fall)), pp. 69–70). John Wiley and Sons.

Taranath, A. (2019). *Beyond guilt trips: Mindful travel in an unequal world.* Between the Lines.

University of Dayton. (n.d.). *Mission and identity.* Retrieved September 12, 2020, from https://udayton.edu/about/mission-and-identity.php

University of Dayton Center for Social Concern. (n.d.). *CSC mission statement.* Retrieved September 12, 2020 from https://udayton.edu/ministry/csc/about.php

Whitehead, D. M. (2015). Global service learning: Addressing the big challenges. *AAC&U Diversity and Democracy, 18.*

World Synod of Catholic Bishops. (1971). *Justicia in Mundo.* Retrieved from https://www.cctwincities.org/wp-content/uploads/2015/10/Justicia-in-Mundo.pdf

Supporting Student Development Through Mentorship and Reflection

Nurturing Learning Through the Pre-clinical Music Therapy Supervision Relationship

Joy Willenbrink-Conte

MUSIC THERAPY BACKGROUND

Music therapy, as defined by Bruscia with input from music therapists around the world, is "a reflexive process wherein the therapist helps the client to optimize the client's health using various facets of music experience and the relationships formed through them as the impetus for change" (2014, p. 36). As healthcare, music therapy may address musical, physical, emotional, social, cognitive, and spiritual dimensions of holistic health, and take place in schools, hospitals, treatment centers and clinics, community centers, prisons, and elder care settings, as well as in the homes of music therapy clients or participants[1] (AMTA, 2020). Music therapy

[1] While the term client is often utilized to describe an individual seeking or receiving therapy services, not all individuals in this situation have with their own choice and agency sought treatment. In situations such as residential care, individuals may actually have minimal capacity to assert their preferences for treatment. Therefore, I often use the term therapy

J. Willenbrink-Conte (✉)
Music, University of Dayton, Dayton, OH, USA
e-mail: jwillenbrink1@udayton.edu

© The Author(s), under exclusive license to Springer Nature
Switzerland AG 2022
K. Lovett (ed.), *Diverse Pedagogical Approaches to Experiential Learning, Volume II*,
https://doi.org/10.1007/978-3-030-83688-7_11

gained recognition as an established profession in the US during the mid-twentieth century (Davis & Hadley, 2015). And yet, music in support of health is not unique to the music therapy profession. Throughout history and across the globe, one can find poignant examples of music's healing capacities. For instance, consider the community and social connection possible through participation in a Javanese Gamelan ensemble (Tan et al., 2020), or the emotional regulation, stress relief, and social and cultural resilience activated through the Yoik singing tradition of the Sami, indigenous peoples residing in northern parts of Norway, Finland, Sweden, and Russia (Hämäläinen et al., 2018). To make and experience music is truly an enriching and health-activating human experience.

Music therapy is an experiential form of therapy, meaning the health-oriented transformation comes about through *experiencing* music in roles as listener, creator, or both and, relating with self, the therapist, and/or other client participants. Therefore, music therapy students need varied and ongoing opportunities to experience firsthand health-related challenges and affordances of different music experiences as well as opportunities to practice facilitating such music experiences (Bruscia, 2013). This occurs via various forms of experiential learning (EL) to strengthen self-awareness and improve clinical reflexivity, or capacity to engage as a flexible, responsive, and self-reflective practitioner (Bruscia, 2013; Hiller et al., 2020; Kolb, 2015; Moon, 2004).

SITUATING SELF AND THIS CHAPTER

I composed this chapter during my third year as a lecturer of music therapy and my eighth year as a music therapist. I identify as a white, abled, cisgender woman with considerable privilege and power related to these identities and my educational background, credentialed status, and US citizenship. I began supervising student music therapists two years into my professional music therapy journey. At the time, while I enjoyed the process immensely, I also felt cautious and fearful that I was ill-equipped to provide adequate support to developing clinicians during this important period in their training. In the years that followed, I have supervised many more students. My respect for the nature of the supervision relationship

participant, to describe individuals who have chosen to participate in music therapy treatment, whether or not they sought these services independently. This terminology also underscores my belief that therapy is a partnership between music therapist and participant(s).

has grown, and I recognize a personal need for ongoing learning. Indeed, I am both a supervisor and supervisee (student), as well as an expert and learner.

Given my identities, I bear similarities with the majority of music therapists in the US who, according to the most recent American Music Therapy Association Workforce Analysis (AMTA, 2018), also are overwhelmingly white and female.[2] As such, one can assume that I also bear similarities with the majority of music therapy supervisors in the US, although there are no available demographic statistics. If music therapy is to expand, diversify, and grow beyond the constraints of our history as a field molded by white, ableist, sexist, Eurocentric, and heteronormative ideals, our supervision practices must evolve. Supervisors must be willing to acknowledge their power, and take action to both prevent harm in the form of emotional and psychological distress and support student agency and self-empowerment, particularly when students experience systemic oppression.

I am by no means the first supporter of antiracist, culturally responsive, feminist, and strengths-based supervision practices. I have benefitted from the labor of the many pioneering music therapists referenced throughout this chapter. In what follows, I provide theoretical groundwork, share some of my supervision experiences, and advocate strategies that I believe deepen learning opportunities for both students and supervisors. Considering the myriad demands when facilitating EL, particularly EL involving some form of mentoring or supervision, I hope this chapter might contribute to reader self-reflection, and commitment to evolve one's personal supervision or mentoring style, as well as related systems in one's respective field, to prevent harm and expand learning affordances.

---

[2] The demographics surveyed included age, gender, and ethnicity. Most survey responses came from members of the AMTA professional organization, yet not all music therapists are members of this professional organization as participation is voluntary and requires payment of annual dues. It should be noted that this survey, while requesting information about "gender", used biological sex identifiers of "male" and "female" rather than gender identifiers of man and woman. Additionally, "transgender" was indicated as a separate category, which decreases clarity since many transgender individuals identify as women or men. Thus, it seems that understanding of respondent gender identities may be limited or inaccurate.

Music Therapy Supervision

Supervision is perhaps the most important component in the development of a competent practitioner. It is within the context of supervision that trainees begin to develop a sense of their professional identity and to examine their own beliefs and attitude regarding clients and therapy. (Corey et al., 2007, p. 360)

Role of Pre-clinical Training in Music Therapy Education

Pre-clinical training is a foundational component of music therapy education and involves processes of student observation of supervisor-led sessions, co-facilitation with the supervisor, and, finally, independent session facilitation (AMTA, 2017). Integrated throughout the training program, pre-clinical training precedes the music therapy clinical internship which is more extensive and completed at the conclusion of the training program.[3] Ideally, pre-clinical training enables students to strengthen their clinical skills and practical wisdom—that is, deepening their capacities to *be* with others, connecting personally and musically to support growth.

At the University of Dayton, students participate in five scaffolded semesters of pre-clinical training, each in a different setting with individuals with varied health needs and resources. Students confront a spectrum of personal and clinical challenges and opportunities, and experience intrapersonal, interpersonal, intramusical, intermusical, and ecological relationships. *Intra*—references relationships within the self. Students encounter *intramusical* relationships or situations wherein they explore connections between self and their music (Bruscia, 2014). Perhaps most salient throughout pre-clinical training are *interpersonal* and *intermusical* relationships, or those relationships that exist between self and another, or between the music of self and the music of another (Bruscia, 2014). Lastly, *ecological* relationships are those that occur between an individual or group and a broader context, such as a therapy group, community, network, culture, or system, and those values, norms, beliefs, and power structures that function within the context (Bruscia, 2014).

---

[3] Pre-clinical training hours must total at least 180, and internship hours at least 900, with the sum total training hours resulting in at least 1200 (AMTA, 2017).

STUDENT-SUPERVISOR RELATIONSHIP

> Embarking on internship, for both supervisor and intern is like boarding a small, intimate vessel that cannot sail without the full involvement of two barely acquainted travelers. Waves come from all directions. Each traveler is dependent upon the other, for if one leans forward, lets out sail, or changes direction, the other will feel this, and will need to decide how to respond. Each journey is unique and the ocean is full of challenges, from within and without. (Feiner, 2019, p. 157)

While this imagery is employed to depict the intimacy and interconnectedness of an internship relationship, I believe the same applies to the pre-clinical supervision relationship. In some ways, the risks posed during pre-clinical supervision are greater since these students are earlier in their academic careers than interns. A harmful experience during pre-clinical training could derail a student's progress toward the completion of a clinical degree—returning to the above metaphor—the student could be tossed overboard.

The labels describing the relationship between student and supervisor immediately suggest a power hierarchy. The student is connoted as the learner, whose role is to absorb knowledge and benefit from the expertise of the supervisor, while the supervisor is connoted as the expert, able to oversee and differentiate between poor and best clinical practices. What I will explore below presents a disintegration of this formal hierarchy toward a more mutual relationship wherein both student and supervisor are recognized as learners and experts in particular areas. This approach is aligned with ideals of feminist supervision, which is "process-oriented" (Porter, 1995), collaborative (Porter & Vasquez, 1997), and addresses power differentials (Hewson, 1999). Hahna and Forinash describe feminist supervision as embodied by "multiple perspectives, respect, and embracing a not-knowing approach" (2019, p. 71). In espousing a feminist supervision style, the supervisor commits to ongoing learning and fosters a relationship wherein the student feels empowered to employ and grow the resources they possess. From a feminist perspective, in order to deepen EL, supervisors, mentors, and practitioners are called upon to continue personal learning and reflect carefully on the degree to which each student needs guidance and support versus agency and opportunities for self-guided learning.

Different Types of Student-Supervisor Relationships

Differing and, at times, dual relationships may exist between student and supervisor, as supervisors potentially fulfill other roles within a student's music therapy education and training. For instance, the supervisor may also be a former, current, or future course instructor. I'll term this supervisor status *instructor-supervisor*. In other situations, a supervisor may be, first and foremost, a clinician, engaged in pre-clinical training supervision in an adjunctive capacity. I'll term this status *clinician-supervisor*. Clinician-supervisors are unlikely to hold previous relationships with students, but are certainly likely to work alongside the student in a professional capacity in the future. As a pre-clinical training supervisor, I have worked with students both as an instructor-supervisor and as a clinician-supervisor, and note that the relationships differed.

As an instructor-supervisor, the initial level of trust often mirrors any rapport developed in the classroom, and developing mutuality in the supervision relationship is challenged by the pronounced power differentials between instructors and students that are commonplace in academic settings. For instance, I use my first name in clinical interactions to nurture equality and respect in the relationship, just as I refer to therapy participants by their first name or preferred title. Thus, as an instructor-supervisor, I use my first name in the clinical field. This can place students in an awkward situation as they attempt to call me by my first name in the clinical context but revert to using the title "professor" in alternate academic contexts. I also find this degree of code-switching between my clinician and academic instructor personas cumbersome and disingenuous at times.

I am not advocating for one type of supervisor relationship over the other. I have had experiences where strong trust and mutuality were achieved in relationship with students as an instructor-supervisor. In contrast, I have had difficulty developing rapport and mutuality in relationship with students as a clinician-supervisor. Yet, these supervisory relationship dynamics do differ and can significantly impact learning experiences. Relational factors such as these should be considered and, I believe, discussed by students and supervisors (as well as by EL practitioners more broadly) to promote healthy communication, boundaries, and working alliances.

STUDENT AND SUPERVISOR IDENTITIES AND RELATIONAL DYNAMICS

Above, I've indicated that a power differential exists intrinsically in supervision relationships, and noted the ways in which supervisor roles may shape the nature of the relationship. Likewise, unique relational dynamics can be activated by many other student and supervisor identities and the intersections of these identities, including race, ethnic heritage, gender identity, presentation, and expression, age, degree of being abled and/or disabled by the situation and context, sexual orientation, language(s), credentials or lack thereof, educational background, class, religious affiliation, spiritual beliefs and practices, or lack thereof, body shape and size, and communication and learning styles, among others.

Whitehead-Pleaux (2019) and Swamy and Kim (2019) write about culturally responsive music therapy supervision and the ways in which these supervisory practices represent a divergence from traditional supervision models in the field of music therapy. Culturally responsive supervision demands that the supervisors examine themselves, commit to learning about different cultures, and make changes to invite conversations about power, privilege, and oppression into the relationship. With deepened perspectives, the supervisor alters their clinical and supervisory practices accordingly (Whitehead-Pleaux, 2019). Swamy and Kim (2019) further explain that to be culturally responsive is to be strengths-based when it comes to recognizing, affirming, and empowering student identities as resources in the clinical context.

Norris and Hadley (2019) indicate that acknowledgment of race and exploration of racial oppression and power dynamics are often avoided in clinical, and specifically, music therapy supervision when supervisors "adopt a color-evasive ideology" (p. 103) to minimize personal discomfort, despite the harm inflicted upon students (Burkard et al., 2016). Norris and Hadley assert that music therapy as a discipline conforms to white, Eurocentric norms, while simultaneously avoiding affirmation of racial differences and values, and often failing to consider the racialized systems that impact health. These authors champion supervision strategies that are antiracist—involving the recognition of race-based oppression and action to dismantle these oppressive forces.

For pre-clinical supervision to be antiracist, culturally responsive, feminist, and strengths-based, the supervisor must (a) hold awareness of power dynamics, and take action to minimize imbalance and increase mutuality;

(b) validate student and supervisor intersectional identities and how identities do or do not overlap with those of therapy participants; and (c) honor and help amplify the strengths and resources students possess, particularly their unique perspectives.

STUDENT-SUPERVISOR-SETTING RELATIONSHIPS

In pre-clinical supervision, there is not only a relationship between supervisor and student, but also relationships formed with the therapy participant(s) and the contexts in which therapy takes place. In music therapy, this web of relationships is deepened and enriched by relationships formed in and around music, weaving a complex and nuanced tapestry. Likewise, these dense webs of relationships exist anytime EL is community situated.

ECOLOGICAL FACTORS

Therapy does not happen in a vacuum. Music therapy practice is impacted by socio-cultural notions of health and music. Each context for therapy, whether it be a school, private clinic, prison, or rehabilitation center, is shaped by external ecological forces (e.g., geographic location and streams of funding), as well as internal ecological forces (e.g., institutional culture, norms, values, beliefs, and power structures). Acknowledging and exploring the impacts of these ecological forces in supervision benefits learning. For instance, in my work with students completing pre-clinical training in mental health care settings, I find it immensely meaningful to have conversations about the stigmatization of individuals with mental illnesses and addictions, while social and community health resources for these persons are poor and frequently inaccessible. This social landscape in conjunction with any personal or familial experiences with mental illness and addiction undoubtedly shapes our perspectives and belief systems. Without opportunities to explore these personal and socio-cultural lenses, hidden byproducts may surface and strain or inhibit therapeutic progress.

I have experienced instances of strong alignment with, as well as stark rejection of the ecological forces that exerted pressure on music therapy practice; so too have the students with whom I have been privileged to work. In instances when students express their discomfort with and ultimately reject particular norms and values of a treatment institution, it could be easy to adopt a defensive stance. Rather, the supervisor has an opportunity to grow by listening and learning from student perspectives. In my experience, student confrontation of harmful systems, even when student views aligned with my own, made me aware of situations when I had remained silent and maintained the status quo. In doing so, I caused immediate harm and perpetuated systemic oppression, often in the form of ableism, cissexism, heterosexism, and white supremacy. Student action and assertive communication helped to yield both systemic and personal changes.

I reflect on one such instance with Noah,[4] a pre-clinical training student who later completed his clinical internship with me at the same hospital. Noah spoke up about his discomfort surrounding the treatment team intake process at our hospital. During these intake meetings, an individual new to the hospital would meet members of their treatment team: the psychiatrist, social worker, a nursing staff person, and me as the primary therapist. This process was designed to allow all treatment parties an expeditious way to complete their required intake assessment documentation while preventing the individuals from having to repeat themselves in responding to particular assessment questions. However, residents frequently described the experience as threatening because several unfamiliar people rapidly asked intimate and complex questions. Additionally, although the room was meant to be a private space, other staff frequently barged in unknowingly, interrupting the process, and undoubtedly impacting the individual's experience of safety and security. I found the nature of these intake meetings to be problematic, and certainly neither person-centered nor demonstrative of patience or respect as the individual transitioned onto the treatment unit. Therefore, I typically joined for these team intake meetings, but completed my assessment process individually, in a private space on the treatment unit rather than in a staff office. I found this allowed me to build rapport and more readily individualize the assessment.

Following one such team intake meeting, Noah spoke up to indicate that he perceived the process as non-therapeutic and potentially harmful. I immediately agreed. His reactions aligned with my own, and yet, what had I truly done to attempt to change this problematic process? Rather than assertively address my colleagues to acknowledge my concerns and prioritize resident care and safety, I had merely attempted to model better

---

[4] My sincere gratitude goes to Noah Lucas, MT-BC, for granting permission to include this vignette and reviewing for accuracy.

behavior while remaining silent and, thus, complicit. After Noah spoke up, I felt compelled to address my colleagues more directly. His bold willingness to confront this issue in our dialogue motivated me to take necessary action. Students engaged in EL ought to have opportunities to learn about, as well as critique, the systems and norms at play during their learning experiences. Supervisors, mentors, and practitioners should therefore be mindful to enrich rather than inhibit such action.

THERAPY PARTICIPANT IDENTITIES

Supervision relationships wherein students and supervisors explore their personal intersectional identities lay the groundwork for exploring the effects of therapist and therapy participant identities on rapport building, interpersonal and intermusical relationships, as well as assessment, treatment planning, and evaluation processes. Additionally, topics such as racism, sexism, and ableism arise in the clinical context, and therapists must have the necessary resources to navigate these conversations in ways that honor their importance and significance in connection with health and well-being.

Certainly, clinical contexts are not the only spaces where identities of involved participants impact relationships. In fact, I would argue that most EL, particularly learning situated in community contexts, demands consideration of personal and partner identities. Students should have ongoing support in this developmental realm. EL supervisors and practitioners can first and foremost model commitment to ongoing intrapersonal learning, self-assessment, and practices of cultural reflexivity, and can intentionally create space for learning and action to foster cultural reflexivity and erode systems of oppression.

To illustrate, I reflect on my work with Sam and Camille as an instructor-supervisor. We facilitated music therapy with a men's group in a residential addiction treatment center, and created an open and honest platform at the onset of the semester to discuss power dynamics related to race and gender. We entered the clinical space with significant power due to our health statuses, whiteness, class, and access to educational resources, while the group members presented with power due to identifying as men while we each identified as women. Together during our regular post-session debriefing, we discussed manifestations of power and oppression. I shared my insights, perspectives, and strategies I've used to navigate similar occurrences in the past. I also honestly acknowledged that there is no "rule-book" for music therapy, which is always a unique phenomenon shaped by the people, music, and ecologies involved. Consistent with practices of self-guided, self-controlled, or self-directed learning (King, 2011; Simons, 2000), I encouraged Sam and Camille to find approaches that aligned with their values when confronting oppression and wisely wielding their power during clinical encounters.

In what follows, Camille[5] explores the role of supervision after a group member uses a slur during a session: *While working as a student music therapist with a group of men in an inpatient addiction center, I became increasingly aware of how the world I live in varied from many of the men in the group. It was through supervision that I came to realize, accept, and challenge my own views of the world, music therapy, and the men – who offered me opportunities to learn and grow through and surrounding the music we shared.*

One of the most challenging and impactful moments was when one man used the ableist term, "retarded". This particular experience left me speechless and numb. As someone who considers themselves to be an advocate for individuals with disabilities, when this word is used, I often respectfully explain how and why certain words or phrases may be hurtful or harmful to certain individuals. However, when I heard this man say "retarded", I froze. I had a thousand thoughts going through my mind, yet, I didn't know how to respond, so, I didn't. Following the session, I felt disappointed in myself, but also angry with the individual who said that word. It was through the support of my supervisor and practicum partner that I came to realize how important it is to express one's own discomforts or to challenge ideas if they may affect the dynamic of a group or the work between client and therapist. My own experiences and emotions related to the use of the term "retarded" are important, but I think it goes beyond that. Through debriefing, I was able to talk through my own personal relationship with the word, but also realize how it may affect someone else in the group. As the therapist, I may have the voice that someone else wished they could use. Therefore, the point might not be to call anyone out for saying something I deemed as disrespectful, but to make sure everyone in the group feels as comfortable and understood as possible, therapist included.

---

[5] My sincere gratitude goes to Camille Bagnola, music therapy intern, for contributing this written reflection.

Just as future or current music therapists often lend a listening ear to the individuals we engage with in therapy, it is important for us to have the same opportunity. Supervision has been invaluable, and gives me the chance to receive immediate feedback on current and future sessions, further process my own emotions and thoughts, and collaborate with someone who may have different insights as to what may best benefit me as a future therapist, as well as the individuals I serve.

Here, Sam[6] examines how supervision supported her capacity to musically affirm Black group members: *I don't think our work could have been nearly as impactful without the strong and open relationship we developed as a treatment team. Our intentional reflection time was essential to my learning and growth as a student music therapist. While I agree that gender identity often impacted our work and some sexist interactions within sessions required deep reflection throughout the semester, I think that navigating the cultural and clinical considerations related to our Black group members required even further reflection, and for which supervision was certainly supportive. When I reflect on my needs during supervision this particular semester, I remember how important it felt to have a space to safely and openly consider ways in which race and culture impacted our group. Frequent and deep thinking as a treatment team seemed to help us find ways to affirm Black group members within a group where the majority of members were white. This experience helped me to deeply consider the many ways in which race and culture can impact therapeutic and group relationships.*

These accounts describe just a few of the complex, nuanced, and emotionally activating ways in which therapist and therapy participant identities impact therapy. As such, supervision is a vital context for debriefing, dialogue, support, and learning, and demands supervisor investment.

ROLE OF MUSIC AND MUSICAL IDENTITIES

Music is an ever-present force in music therapy. The music itself, shared or created by participants and therapists, functions as an agent of change—nurturing growth, creating new pathways, and unlocking potentials. Likewise, the musical identities of all individuals engaged in music therapy and the intramusical and intermusical relationships formed throughout the process can catalyze health-oriented change. Just as the music

---

[6] My sincere gratitude goes to Sam Roane, music therapy student, for contributing this written reflection.

therapist gets to know the musical selfhood of therapy participants, the supervisor meets and relates to the musical self of the student, and vice versa.

To illustrate this, I reflect on my experience as a clinician-supervisor with Khyla in the context of pre-clinical training at an inpatient mental health hospital.[7] Near the conclusion of one particular session, a few residents spoke up about their love of bachata music and artists. Although I was unfamiliar with this genre of music, Khyla immediately and enthusiastically bonded with several group members over a shared love of bachata. Khyla's musical personhood enabled her to validate group member music identities in a deeper and more authentic fashion than I was able. In this encounter, Khyla was certainly the expert and I the learner.

STRATEGIES TO DEEPEN SUPERVISION RELATIONSHIPS AND LEARNING

Drawn from the supervision theories outlined above and my experiences, I believe the following strategies help to foster safe and healthy supervision relationships as well as expand intrapersonal and interpersonal learning. I also suggest that these strategies are beneficial in a range of EL contexts.

ACKNOWLEDGE, VALIDATE, AND EXPLORE DIFFERENT IDENTITIES AND ECOLOGIES

To truly deepen intrapersonal and interpersonal learning during supervision, supervisors must (a) acknowledge their own, their students', and therapy participants' differing identities, (b) validate the richness that individuals with different identities and correspondingly diverse perspectives bring to therapy and supervision relationships, and (c) create space in supervision for exploring intersectionality. This is not to say that all identities of student and supervisor ought to be exposed and explored during supervision. However, the supervisor can model self-reflection and nurture an environment wherein the student both reflects on their identities and also considers the intersections and clinical influences of these identities.

---

[7] My sincere gratitude goes to Khyla Anderson, MT-BC, for granting permission to include this vignette and reviewing for accuracy.

Different individuals inhabit different ecologies depending on the cultures with which they identify and those within which they are positioned. Likewise, we are all impacted differently by ecological forces. Supervision grants an opportunity to explore broad and specific ecological relationships, and develop means of adjusting clinical practice accordingly. Such awareness can contribute to a shift in perspective, away from a hyper-focus on individual disorder or disease, and instead toward ecological illness and the need to support healing and wellness within systems, cultures, or communities.

PRACTICE HEALTHY COMMUNICATION AND HONOR STUDENT EXPERTISE

Supervisor commitments to open communication and acceptance of student expressions through deep listening can promote mutuality in the supervision relationship. Healthy and deep listening must involve the supervisor's willingness to accept and witness a student's criticism and anger, and enter into interpersonal spaces that may feel painful or uncomfortable.[8] Ideally, the supervisor modeling these practices might serve to open pathways for students to also embrace critical feedback and be willing to step outside their comfort zones in pivotal moments. Quite often, students are expected to demonstrate these learning strategies while supervisors themselves may show resistance to criticism and personal discomfort.

Supervisor self-disclosure can also create pathways for open communication. I find that students benefit immensely from hearing about not only my expertise, but also my hesitations, limitations, and weaknesses. Honestly acknowledging areas where I need to grow affirms that perfection is indeed unattainable and music therapy practice demands lifelong intrapersonal and intramusical learning. Students are *expected* to develop and mature during clinical training. However, when the supervisor also approaches the experience as an opportunity for growth, they can benefit from the richness of a dynamic and symbiotic student-supervisor relationship. To achieve this symbiosis, Supervisors must acknowledge

---

[8] I state this as a white, cis, abled supervisor with considerable power and privilege. There may certainly be situations wherein student expression of anger is unwarranted and could pose significant harm to the supervisor. In such situations, the supervisor need not expose themself to undue harm, and external support or intervention may be necessary.

student expertise in particular areas, including expertise regarding self, and personal vantage points informed by one's intersectional identities.

COMMIT TO PERSONAL WORK OUTSIDE OF THE SUPERVISION RELATIONSHIP

In many circumstances, supervisors also benefit from supervision, particularly when the student-supervisor dynamics are challenging, or supervisors are relying heavily on their students for education. Indeed, it can be quite burdensome for a student to have to consistently educate their supervisor while also being responsible for their own learning. Marginalized and systemically oppressed students in particular can be heavily taxed by supervisors who rely on them to speak up and confront oppression. Meanwhile, oppressive incidents often cause layered harm to the student. In this context, I am drawing a distinction between honoring student expertise and *relying* on students for education. When supervisors are in the latter position, it indicates their need to seek out personal supervision, and external training, education, and other growth opportunities.

TAKE ACTION WHEN SUPERVISION IS NOT WORKING

Like all other types of relationships, sometimes a supervision relationship simply does not work. As described above, unhealthy supervision relationships run the risk of harming students and supervisors. In these instances, it is important to take action to either resolve problematic dynamics, perhaps with the support of mediation, or dissolve the current supervision relationship and link the student with a better-suited supervisor or treatment context placement. It should also be noted that students tend to have less power in the supervision relationship, and thus may have greater difficulty and fewer resources for alerting their supervisor or an outside advocate that they are being harmed. To minimize harm, channels should be present for students and supervisors to seek mediation, support, and advocacy should problematic situations arise during supervision. These channels ought to be made available systemically to support and protect all parties, including students, supervisors, and therapy participants.

ADAPTATIONS TO OTHER DISCIPLINES AND CONCLUSION

While music therapy pre-clinical supervision certainly represents a unique phenomenon, considerations drawn from clinical supervisory practices can be applied to situations of supervision, mentorship, and EL in other fields, particularly when community or external partners are involved. Through such learning relationships, there is an opportunity for students and instructors to flex—moving beyond rigid roles of learner and expert—in order to confront the unique challenges and opportunities that arise, and experience the interpersonal richness possible when relationships are formed between two or more people with different life experiences and worldviews (Beard & Wilson, 2018; Moon, 2004). Additionally, when working with community partners, supervisors bear the awesome responsibility to model the formation of just and balanced partnerships that are co-constructed with an understanding of the voices, needs, and resources of all those involved (Cone & Payne, 2002; Leiderman et al., 2002). As students and supervisors engage in relationships with one another, community participants, and community sites, the spectrum of interpersonal and ecological relationships can spark otherwise inaccessible intrapersonal learning. This deepened self-awareness, in turn, affords richer future interpersonal and ecological learning. What a beautiful cycle to nurture!

REFERENCES

American Music Therapy Association (AMTA). (2017). *Standards for education and clinical training.* https://www.musictherapy.org/members/edctstan/

AMTA. (2018). *2018 AMTA workforce analysis and member survey.* https://www.musictherapy.org/assets/1/7/18WorkforceAnalysis.pdf

AMTA. (2020). *How to find a music therapist.* https://www.musictherapy.org/about/find/

Beard, C., & Wilson, J. P. (2018). *Experiential learning: A practical guide for training, coaching, and education.* Kogan Page.

Bruscia, K. (2013). Self-experiences in the pedagogy of music therapy. In K. Bruscia (Ed.), *Music therapy education, training, and supervision* (pp. 16–34). Barcelona Publishers.

Bruscia, K. (2014). *Defining music therapy* (3rd ed.). Barcelona Publishers.

Burkard, A. W., Edwards, L. M., & Adams, H. A. (2016). Racial color blindness in counseling, therapy, and supervision. In H. A. Neville, M. E. Gallardo, & D. W. Sue (Eds.), *The myth of racial color blindness: Manifestations, dynamics, and impact* (pp. 294–311). American Psychological Association.

Cone, D., & Payne, P. (2002). When campus and community collide: Campus-community partnerships from a community perspective. *The Journal of Public Affairs, 6*(1), 203–218.

Corey, G., Corey, M. S., & Callanan, P. (2007). *Issues and ethics in the helping professions* (7th ed.). Thompson Brooks/Cole.

Davis, W., & Hadley, S. (2015). A history of music therapy. In B. Wheeler (Ed.), *Music therapy handbook* (pp. 17–28). The Guilford Press.

Feiner, S. (2019). A journey through internship supervision revisited: Roles, dynamics, and phases of the supervisory relationship. In M. Forinash (Ed.), *Music therapy supervision* (2nd ed., pp. 157–176). Barcelona Publishers.

Hahna, N., & Forinash, M. (2019). Feminist approaches to supervision. In M. Forinash (Ed.), *Music therapy supervision* (2nd ed., pp. 59–73). Barcelona Publishers.

Hämäläinen, S., Musial, F., Salamonsen, A., Graff, O., & Olsen, T. A. (2018). Sami yoik, Sami history, Sami health: A narrative review. *International Journal of Circumpolar Health, 77*(1). https://doi.org/10.1080/2242398 2.2018.1454784

Hewson, D. (1999). Empowerment in supervision. *Feminism & Psychology, 9*, 406–409.

Hiller, J., Belt, C., Gardstrom, S., & Willenbrink-Conte, J. (2020). Safeguarding curricular self-experiences in undergraduate music therapy education and training. *Music Therapy Perspectives.* https://academic.oup.com/mtp/advance-article/doi/10.1093/mtp/miaa027/6056236?guestAccessKey=d 3e4295a-dcd8-4b38-93fd-498330de8dbb

King, C. (2011). Fostering self-directed learning through guided tasks and learner reflection. *Studies in Self-Access Learning Journal, 2*(4), 257–267.

Kolb, D. (2015). *Experiential learning: Experience as the source of learning and development.* Pearson Education, Inc.

Leiderman, S. A., Furco, A., Zapf, J. A., & Goss, M. (2002). *Building partnerships with college campuses: Community perspectives.* A Publication of the Consortium for the Advancement of Private Higher Education's Engaging Communities and Campuses Grant Program. http://ncsce.net/wpcontent/uploads/2016/04/BuildingPartnershipsWithCollegeCampuses-CommuniityPerspectives.pdf

Moon, J. A. (2004). *A handbook of reflective and experiential learning: Theory and practice.* Routledge Falmer.

Norris, M., & Hadley, S. (2019). Engaging race in music therapy supervision. In M. Forinash (Ed.), *Music therapy supervision* (2nd ed., pp. 101–125). Barcelona Publishers.

Porter, N. (1995). Supervision of psychotherapists: Integrating anti-racist, feminist, and multicultural perspectives. In H. Landrine (Ed.), *Bringing cultural diversity to feminist psychology: Theory, research, and practice.* American Psychological Association.

Porter, N., & Vasquez, N. (1997). Covision: Feminist supervision, process, and collaboration. In J. Worell & N. G. Johnson (Eds.), *Shaping the future of feminist psychology: Education, research, and practice.* American Psychological Association.

Simons, R.-J. (2000). Various kinds of life long learning. In F. Achtenhagen & W. Lempert (Eds.), *Lebenslanges Lernen im Beruf—seine Grundlegung im Kindes- und Jugendalter [Lifelong learning in the vocations. Its foundations in infancy and adolescence]* (Vol. 4, pp. 23–38). Leske und Budrich.

Summer, L. (2019). Supervision of first-time practicum. In M. Forinash (Ed.), *Music therapy supervision* (2nd ed., pp. 129–140). Barcelona Publishers.

Swamy, S., & Kim, S.-A. (2019). Culturally responsive academic supervision in music therapy. In M. Forinash (Ed.), *Music therapy supervision* (2nd ed., pp. 217–238). Barcelona Publishers.

Tan, L., Tjoeng, J., & Sin, H. X. (2020). "Ngeli": Flowing together in a Gamelan ensemble. *Psychology of Music.* https://doi.org/10.1177/0305735620909482

Whitehead-Pleaux, A. (2019). Culturally responsive music therapy supervision. In M. Forinash (Ed.), *Music therapy supervis* (2nd ed., pp. 45–58). Barcelona Publishers.

CHAPTER 12

Assigning Reflection in Experiential Learning for Professional Formation

Denise Platfoot Lacey

Over the many years I have taught a credit-bearing externship course at a law school, I have read hundreds, if not thousands, of reflective memos in which my students have shared the most important things they learned in their legal externships and how the use of deliberate reflective practice enhanced their emerging professional identities. However, student appreciation for reflective practice in experiential learning (EL) often develops slowly over the course of the semester. Students must learn how reflective practice can strengthen their experience, why it is a critical part of EL, and how it can help them develop their identities as members of the legal profession.

These benefits are not always immediately apparent to students, so I work with them to help them develop the skill of reflection and hopefully, an appreciation for it. Consequently, students often come to realize that reflection on their experiences is a valuable element of a professional's practice and that incorporating it into their professional identity will enrich

D. Platfoot Lacey (✉)
School of Law, University of Dayton, Dayton, OH, USA
e-mail: dlacey1@udayton.edu

© The Author(s), under exclusive license to Springer Nature Switzerland AG 2022
K. Lovett (ed.), *Diverse Pedagogical Approaches to Experiential Learning, Volume II*,
https://doi.org/10.1007/978-3-030-83688-7_12

171

them as legal professionals. In this chapter, I will share the insights I have gained about effective ways to facilitate meaningful student reflection in EL and enhance student formation of professional identity.

THE EXTERNSHIP COURSE

At the University of Dayton School of Law, all students are required to take an experiential course in their final year. The externship course satisfies this requirement. As explained by Stuckey (2007), EL courses incorporate actual experience with academic inquiry and self-reflection. Therefore, law students in an externship course act in the role of lawyers and observe practicing lawyers/judges in a legal setting outside of the law school while concurrently evaluating the doctrine and theory underlying their experiences and engaging in reflective practice about their learning. Indeed, students commonly describe this integrated process, as demonstrated by one student's comments:

> I think that the externship is an invaluable experience because I feel like I am learning so much more at work than in the classroom. I am able to see how doctrine actually works in the legal field and understand what goes on 'behind the scenes.'

An externship for course credit is unique from other EL because the actual experience in the field placement serves as the primary method of instruction, rather than it serving as a supplement to the classroom presentation of a subject matter (Stuckey, 2007). Students can undoubtedly experience valuable learning through both of these methods, but in an externship course, the field placement experience is the focus of the course. It is the "text for learning" (Maranville et al., 2015, p. 225).

In my course, students are placed in different types of legal offices where they work part-time for an entire semester. The work must be substantive and educational in nature. As directed by the accrediting standards for law schools, externship fieldwork must include "a substantial lawyering experience that [ ] is reasonably similar to the experience of a lawyer advising or representing a client or engaging in other lawyering tasks in a setting outside a law clinic under the supervision of a licensed attorney or an individual otherwise qualified to supervise" (ABA Standard 304(d)). Lawyering tasks might include drafting legal documents, interacting with clients, preparing for trial, observing court hearings, and the like.

The accrediting standards also require "ongoing, contemporaneous, faculty-guided reflection" (ABA Standard 304(a)(5)) because "optimal learning from experience involves a continuous, circular four stage sequence of experience, reflection, theory, and application" (Stuckey, 2007, p. 122). Structured opportunities for students to reflect on their experiences are key to helping them "distill their understanding of their experiences and prepare to carry the reflection habits forward into practice" (Maranville et al., 2015, p. 225). Despite this, students often do not realize that the structure of the externship course necessarily involves reflective practice until they commence their externship. As one student explained: "My initial perception of critical self-reflection being an integral aspect of this externship course was one of interest and also of curiosity. I have never heard the term before."

Reflective practice is critical to students' ability to transfer their knowledge from the context of their externship fieldwork to other contexts (Griffin, et al., 2010). As students perform the lawyering tasks common in their field placements, students concurrently engage in reflection to consider what they are learning and how they will use it in their legal career, even if it is in a wholly different area of law than their field placement. Simply put by one student:

> These assignments have given me the opportunity to take current experiences and look toward applying them now and, in the future, through my personal and professional life. Engaging in deliberate reflective analysis of my experiences has provided an avenue of internalization of the impact my personal experiences will have on me through my future as a lawyer.

Formation of Professional Identity

Professional education is intended to expose future practitioners to the knowledge, judgment, and defining values of the profession and to provide them opportunities to develop their professional identities (Sullivan et al., 2007). EL, and specifically externships for course credit, is an ideal way to foster the formation of professional identity because they provide intentional opportunities for students to be directly exposed to practitioners doing real work (Maranville et al., 2015). Externships expose students to practice situations that teach them knowledge and skills, but also how those intersect with a lawyer's values (Floyd & Kerew, 2017). As one student observed:

> The externship memos this summer allowed me to take a step back from everything and see the full picture. It is easy to come in and focus solely on the work that you are doing, but fail to see all the "parts of the clock" working together. The memos help you reflect to see the full picture and to see why people act and make decisions how they do and why I make my decisions in the manner that I do.

Studies show that reflective practice effectively fosters professional formation (Hamilton, 2012). Through the guided reflection in externship courses, students "develop their professional identity, improve their professionalism, [and] intensify their ethical sensitivity and self-awareness" (Maranville et al., 2015, p. 232). Since the EL cycle includes intentionally reflecting on the experience, students can begin to unearth the values of the profession and identify their distinct role within it (McLeod, 2017). Students will sometimes identify this as a benefit of the reflective practice in which they are engaged during their externship:

> Critical reflection and self-evaluation are both essential for professional growth and this has been key to my legal and professional enhancement this summer. Throughout the summer, the externship memos have given me an opportunity to reflect on my own attributes, how they are applicable to my career and externship goals, and the extent that they will serve me in my profession as an immigration attorney.

Yet, my experience is that many law students do not initially see the value of purposeful reflection concerning the learning that is taking place in their externships, nor do they always appreciate the importance of self-reflection. Typical comments by students at the beginning of the semester often demonstrate this perspective. For example: "My initial perception of critical self-reflection being an integral aspect of our externship coursework this semester is that it will be a waste of time."

My goal is by the end of a semester of engaging in reflective practice, students can—at a minimum—acknowledge that reflection had a useful purpose in their externship experience and ideally, that it strengthened their learning and is a valuable practice worth integrating into their role as a professional. As sometimes illustrated in end-of-semester reflections, student perceptions of the value of reflection do evolve over time. At the end of one semester, one student said:

> While at first I was wary of the whole "critical reflection" aspect of the externship program, in the end, it was extremely beneficial because it forced me to engage in a type of inner-self-analysis which I, on my own, would not have done. This is a critical part of my growth as an aspiring [ ] attorney because if I am not able to reflect on my ambitions, mistakes, and triumphs then how will I grow? I truly think [the] prompts are engaging and encouraged thoughtful self-reflection that actually made me think about my growth as both a person and a legal advocate.

Because of the importance of reflective practice in externships and growth as a professional, two learning objectives of my course specifically target reflection. They are as follows:

- Students will demonstrate the habits of a reflective practitioner, through reflective analysis and critical thinking about their externship fieldwork, their professional development, and the values, ethics, and professionalism of the legal profession.
- Students will demonstrate the habits of a self-directed learner by taking initiative for their own learning, including setting goals for it, identifying means and strategies to enhance it, and self-evaluating their progress toward it.

Explaining Reflective Practice

I have learned that the presentation of the reflective exercises is equally as important as having meaningful exercises to engage in. Law students consistently question the value of reflective practice in law courses, so I spend a good deal of time at the beginning of the semester explaining—even justifying—why reflection is necessary for EL.

One exercise I use is to show a video which demonstrates the importance of intentional awareness. The video features two teams of basketball players, one dressed in black shirts and the other dressed in white shirts. The video asks viewers to count the number of passes made by the team in white. The players of both teams begin running around making passes to their own team members. After the passing stops, the video tells the viewers that the team in white made 13 passes but asks whether the viewer saw the moonwalking bear. The video then rewinds and replays to show that a person dressed in a black bear costume moonwalked through the center of activity. Because most viewers are intent on counting how many passes the team in white was making, they often do not notice the moonwalking bear. The message at the end of the video reads "It's easy to miss something you're not looking for."

I explain that in an externship it is easy to miss things they are not looking for because growth occurs in unexpected ways. I explain that deliberately reflecting on the experience helps students catch things they may have missed at the moment and that only by catching them can they integrate them into their existing knowledge. I then ask students to re-state in their own words the connection between the moonwalking bear video and reflective practice in the externship course. My experience is that the video edifies for students the importance of reflection. As one student put it:

> The video demonstrates how easy it can be to overlook obvious facts, issues, etc. when one is not paying attention to that particular area. By focusing on one area, another area can be ignored which could lead to inadequate performance, mistakes, and other issues. By critically reflecting on the externship, one will be looking at all aspects of the experience and learning and analyzing each area. In this manner, it will help prevent overlooking certain areas and promote more rounded learning and growth.

Creating Reflective Assignments

I have found that meaningful self-reflection often requires guidance. While free-write reflective journaling can be beneficial, I find that my students usually need focus. Accordingly, in addition to assigning reflection directly related to the work in their field placement, I offer topics and writing prompts that encourage reflection on various distinct aspects of professional identity. I assign topics such as character, communication styles, grit and resiliency, implicit bias, maximizing strengths, personality, professionalism, professional responsibility, teamwork, and time management. These relate to common elements of professional identity that have been identified in foundational studies on professional education (Hamilton, 2012).

Students are permitted to select the topics of their choice to reflect upon at various points throughout the semester. This is important because it allows them to take ownership of their reflective practice by choosing topics that interest them and relate most to their experience. Usually, I provide a link to a free online self-assessment that students can take to learn more about themselves and offer writing prompts that ask the students to connect the topic to the practice of law. Students reflect on how the topic connects to their externship work and how they will use what they learned in the future, particularly when they are practicing lawyers.

For example, one topic is on teamwork. After assigning a self-assessment on team roles, I provide the following prompts to guide student reflection: explain whether the role identified by the assessment fits you. What are the benefits of this role on a team? What challenges do you see arising with this role and how can they be resolved? If you see any of these roles represented by the lawyers/judges in your externship, provide a critique of how they advance or challenge the productivity of teams in your field office. Explain how you can use this role to be effective on teams at your externship and in your ultimate law practice.

MAKING THE REFLECTIVE PROCESS TANGIBLE

Students do not necessarily come to law school proficient in reflective practice. Therefore, we must teach them reflection skills (McNamara & Field, 2007). One student effectively summed up the challenge that some students face when they reflect on their field experience for the first time:

> The actual process of engaging in critical reflection can be difficult at first. Simply because, I think it can be hard to put something like this – an experience – into words. At first it was somewhat frustrating. Sometimes I felt like I was pulling at strings, but once I identified a specific example that I wanted to share, the words came to me.

Since reflection is an intangible process for many students, I provide a method for students to engage in it. I provide a "What? So What? Now What?" framework that can be a step-by-step guide for engaging in reflective practice (Driscoll & Teh, 2001). First, students describe what they learned. I ask students to use examples from their externships to describe this learning. Next, students explain why it is important to them. Finally, they identify ways that they can use it moving forward in their career. This technique gives students a clear pathway to engage in reflection. Additionally, it helps them see how reflection augments their learning and is a practice that they can carry into their legal careers. As one student said:

Overall, the critical reflection component was extremely beneficial. I was pleasantly surprised. I am genuinely going to use these mindful tools in the future. It is amazing how impactful it can be to take time to reflect. A law student life is busy, but now I know the advantage of taking time for myself and reflect on my learning and experiences. Through the many tools I have learned this summer, this is definitely one I am going to take with me in my legal career.

When assessing the quality of students' written self-reflections, I use a rubric with specific criteria that fall into three categories: (1) description and explanation (i.e., What?), (2) meaningfulness of reflection (i.e., So What?), and (3) complexity of connections made (i.e., Now What?). My rubric is on a simple three-point scale: Exceptional (accomplished/exemplary), Satisfactory (meets expectations), and Unsatisfactory (needs development). I use the following criteria:

- The description and use of examples that the student used to introspectively describe the externship experiences and the selected topic;
- The examination of the impact the experience had on the student;
- The introspection and insights the student shared about the development of the student's own knowledge, skills, and values as a result of the experience; and
- The application and internalization of the student's learning to their anticipated future career.

In addition to evaluating the quality of the reflection and the development of this skill, I am intentional about acknowledging the students' message about their learning experience. In my mind, this feedback is separate and distinct from the skill assessment, but equally important to give to students. Because students share personal feelings and thoughts in the reflections, I want them to know my assessment of the *quality* of their reflection is not a judgment of their *perspective* on the actual experience they describe. Accordingly, I give feedback to students on both the quality of their self-reflection based on the rubric and my reaction to the experience they wrote about. I focus my reaction on affirming their perspective, while at the same time sharing my own experiences as they relate to the topic or encouraging deeper reflection on a particular issue.

Conclusion

At the beginning of the semester, I explicitly acknowledge that the work in the field placement is the core of the course because it is where most of the students' learning during the semester occurs. I elaborate that while the field placement work is at the heart of their learning, a student's reflection on that work is sometimes what is transformative. Often by the end of the semester, students voice how important it was to reflect on their performance because it helped them succeed in their externship. Others point out how reflection advanced their professional growth. Still others describe how reflecting on their experience gave them confidence in their abilities to transition to law practice.

When I feel discouraged from trying to convince law students that reflective practice is a valuable exercise as a professional, I am re-energized when students acknowledge how reflective practice played a valuable part in their experience. For example, one student revealed, "The summer externship was a fantastic experience, and the added structure and requirements for reflection added to my professional and personal growth in ways that a simple internship could not do."

Over the years I have identified several tools to help students see the value of reflective practice: explaining the purpose of reflective practice in EL and how it aids professional formation; creating guided reflection prompts for topics relevant to professional identity; and making the reflective process tangible to students. These are tools that teachers in any discipline can use to enhance the EL experience and professional identity of their students.

References

ABA Standards and Rules of Procedure for Approval of Law Schools. (2020–2021). https://www.americanbar.org/groups/legal_education/resources/standards/

Driscoll, J., & Teh, B. (2001). The potential of reflective practice to develop individual orthopaedic nurse practitioners and their practice. *Journal of Orthopaedic Nursing, 5*, 95–103.

Floyd, T. W., & Kerew, K. L. (2017). Marking the path from law student to lawyer: Using field placement courses to facilitate the deliberate exploration of professional identity and purpose. *Mercer Law Review, 68*, 767–832.

Griffin Jr., J.E., Lorenz, G.F., & Mitchell, D. (2010). *A study of outcomes-oriented student reflection during internship: The integrated, coordinated, and reflection based model of learning and experiential education.* University Office. Paper 2. http://scholarsarchive.jwu.edu/univ_office/2

Hamilton, N. (2012). Fostering professional formation (professionalism): Lessons from the Carnegie Foundation's five studies on educating professionals. *Creighton Law Review, 45,* 763–797.

Maranville, D., Radtke Bliss, L., Wilkes Kaas, C., & Sedillo López, A. (Eds.). (2015). *Building on best practices: Transforming legal education in a changing world.* Matthew Bender & Company, Inc.

McLeod, S. A. (2017). *Kolb's learning styles and experiential learning cycles.* Simply Psychology. https://www.simplypsychology.org/learning-kolb.html

McNamara, J., & Field, R. (2007). Designing reflective assessment for workplace learning in legal education. In *Proceedings ATN evaluation and assessment conference.*

Stuckey, R. (2007). *Best practices for legal education: A vision and a road map.* Clinical Legal Education Association.

Sullivan, W. M., Colby, A., Welch Wegner, J., Bond, L., & Shulman, L. S. (2007). *Educating lawyers: Preparation for the profession of law* (The Carnegie Foundation for the Advancement of Teaching). Jossey-Bass.

CHAPTER 13

Encouraging Growth Through Experiential Education: Contributions of a Teacher Educator

Carrie Rogan-Floom

INTRODUCTION

As a faculty member and university liaison, I have the opportunity and responsibility of contributing to the development of future K-12 teachers. Teacher education has a rich history of Experiential Learning (EL), which provides plentiful methods and resources for working with students in the field. In concert with those resources, I have found various support strategies to be instrumental in promoting students' growth as they participate in EL. In this chapter, I provide a brief background on the program in which I work, and I discuss applicable research and frameworks for aligning support strategies to the types of challenges students encounter. I then offer specific strategies that I have found impactful when helping students mitigate intrapersonal, academic, and professional challenges. Students

C. Rogan-Floom (✉)
Teacher Education, University of Dayton, Dayton, OH, USA
e-mail: roganfloomc1@udayton.edu

K. Lovett (ed.), *Diverse Pedagogical Approaches to Experiential Learning, Volume II*,
https://doi.org/10.1007/978-3-030-83688-7_13

also face interpersonal challenges in EL, so I include support strategies for building and maintaining relationships. The chapter ends with reflections on how these strategies and outcomes can be helpful for the onset of new challenges, such as teaching in a pandemic.

PROGRAM BACKGROUND

EL begins year one at the University of Dayton (UD) for students in the Department of Teacher Education, housed within the School of Education and Health Sciences (SEHS). By the time they graduate, students complete over 600 field hours to prepare them for teaching. Students who want to teach grades 7–12, choose Adolescence to Young Adult (AYA) Education, the program in which I teach. I meet AYA students when they take my course and corresponding lab, typically during their junior year. For the lab, students are placed in a secondary classroom with the teacher, clinical educator (CE), present to practice applying in the field what they are learning in the course. Upon successful completion of the course, students apply to student teach during their senior year. In addition to my teaching position, I serve as a university liaison. In that role, I support and evaluate student teachers, and I also foster and sustain reciprocal partnerships between UD and area schools.

EXPERIENTIAL LEARNING FRAMEWORK

I approach my work with the perspective that UD functions within a *Learning Paradigm* (Barr & Tagg, 1995), which provides insight into how learning is viewed and even, as I have experienced, the potential of EL. When an institution of higher education chooses a complex learning paradigm, as opposed to a simplistic instructional paradigm, there is meaningful contrast. Briefly, in an Instructional Paradigm, focus is placed on the process of populating courses and transmitting information to students (Barr & Tagg, 1995; Tagg, 2003). However, teaching is a complex endeavor. Students are diverse in their funds of knowledge, their development, and their learning goals. To address this complexity, a Learning Paradigm does not focus on process; rather, it prioritizes purpose, which is student learning. The following features are valued in a Learning Paradigm: intrinsic learning goals, authentic performance, consistent and interactive feedback, learning in a long-term horizon, and communities of practice (Barr & Tagg, 1995; Tagg, 2003).

One of those features, authentic performance, is realized through EL opportunities offered at UD. Kolb (2015) provides significant research on EL, which emphasizes learning as a holistic process, grounded in experiences; in these experiences, students play an active role in their learning process. He posits that "learning is the process whereby knowledge is created through the transformation of experience" (Kolb, 2015, p. 49). Kolb's Experiential Learning Cycle (1984) explains: students have a new experience, reflect on the experience, use analysis to form an abstract concept, and then apply new knowledge to new situations. The Association for Experiential Education (2020) adds that a new EL experience challenges learners, describing EL as a "challenge and experience followed by reflection leading to learning and growth." What I would argue is missing from these formulas is the articulated need and subsequent guidance for supporting students, appropriately and timely, as they work through any challenges to realize the growth possible in EL.

There are common challenges that my students face, and I have selected coordinating support strategies informed by the Learning Paradigm (Fig. 13.1). To begin, the AYA program has been carefully designed for *authentic performance,* as students participate in *long-term learning* through aligned and scaffolded teaching and learning activities, all aimed to prepare them for a future career in education. Students complete these activities in community. While working in community is already a core tenet of UD, once part of the AYA team, students become aware that they are now members of a specialized *Learning Community.* To strengthen

Fig. 13.1 Illustration of support strategies in relationship to each other. (Learning paradigm values appear in darker font)

the community, we spend much time on relationship-building and consulting with experts. Students benefit from *consistent and interactive* feedback on their work from multiple stakeholders throughout the program. By first practicing with authentic instruments in low-risk situations, students become comfortable with pushing the boundaries of what they know and taking risks with their learning. Beyond community support, students need strategies to sustain *intrinsic goals* as well. I encourage students to take care of their mental health using such strategies as mindfulness, self-care, and coping ahead. When faced with a challenge, I utilize guiding questions to help them reach a solution. I also provide them with ample opportunities to reflect, not only on how they are coping, but also to note how they are making sense of what they are learning. Certainly, this is not an exhaustive list of supports; it is the best hits collection, and I do find myself adding to it as needed.

Aligned, Accessible Support Strategies Add Potential to Students' Experience

When placed in EL experiences, there are complex demands made upon students as they perform simultaneous tasks with real-world consequences. If students do not have the capacity to meet the demands, they must grow their capacity. The aforementioned EL growth formula is a complex process but is strengthened by the addition of appropriate and timely support strategies. My emphasis on support strategies derives from Constructive Development Theory. There are three premises in Constructive Developmental Theory; one maintains:

> constructivism is the use of cognitive, affective, interpersonal, and intrapersonal capacities to construct and make meaning from experience. The second concept, developmentalism, is based on the premise that, with the appropriate opportunities and challenges, the means through which adults construct and make meaning can change over the life course. Third is subject-object balance. (Mahler, 2011, p. 203)

Subject-object balance is a focus of Kegan's (1982, 1994) orders of consciousness, which accounts for a person's increasing complexity. Kegan's (1994) fourth-order is of interest for college-age students because it includes *self-authorship*, likened to psychological independence. Based on her research with young adults, Baxter Magolda (2007) defines self-authorship as the "internal capacity to define one's own belief system, identity, and relationships" (p. 69). There are several strategies used to promote self-authorship. Kegan (1994) used a bridge-building metaphor to illustrate the need for building a support structure as students cross from one order to a more developed one. Examining challenges and aligning them with appropriate support strategies promotes growth in students and develops their capacity to perform in their EL role.

THE IMPORTANCE OF STUDENTS' INTRAPERSONAL, ACADEMIC, AND PROFESSIONAL DEVELOPMENT

EL, specifically here the act of teaching, is hard work; it makes demands of students' time, mental capacity, energy, social life, and heart. And at age 21, those are especially daunting demands, but my students are eager to take on this good work. By the time that I meet them, they have successfully completed many of their education courses and some field experience, but they are anticipating the next step on the path to become a secondary teacher. What they are not quite prepared for are the challenges that await them in their senior year: the sleepless nights, the fun college student activities that they will inevitably have to miss, the complex lives of their teenage students, the pressure to continuously produce quality work, the prolific constructive criticism they receive, and the transformation from a college student to a professional while still living as a college student. There is much growth that happens somewhere between when I see them enter the door in their sweatpants, logo t-shirts, bed head, and flip flops and when I see them in their trouser pants, blouses, gelled updos, new accessories, and shiny shoes. What happens during that transition is exciting, monumental, life-changing, and sometimes painful. They have intense expectations placed on them, but they can benefit and grow because of these expectations; that is my goal for them.

Parker Palmer (2007) described teaching as "emerg(ing) from one's inwardness, for better or worse...teaching holds a mirror to the soul" (p. 2). If students are not given the space and encouragement to explore and reconcile the demands placed on them, their teaching performance can serve as a source of soul discontent, sometimes even taxing their mental health and leaving them to question their decision to become a teacher. In addition, people around them could become the recipients of the negative effects of their disconnect:

> knowing my students and my subject depends heavily on self-knowledge. When I do not know myself, I cannot know who my students are...I cannot know my subject—not at the deepest levels of embodied, personal meaning. I will know it only abstractly, from a distance, a congeries of concepts as far removed from the world as I am from personal truth. (Palmer, 2007, p. 3)

While it may seem obvious why it is important to have a healthy sense of self, helping students to do that can be a quite involved process.

SUPPORTING STUDENTS STRUGGLING WITH INTRAPERSONAL DEMANDS

Students can become overwhelmed, anxious, stressed, or even disconnected due to the demands placed on them. Starting junior year, before my students even begin student teaching, I talk to them about ways to prepare and *cope ahead* (Linehan, 2015) for future challenges. I routinely utilize the time at the beginning of class to check-in with students and ask them to identify and share how they are feeling. When students are feeling anxious, for example, we discuss possible actions and outcomes, ultimately deciding upon a plan. In addition, I ask students at the beginning of the semester to make a list of activities that provide them comfort and reduce stress. Commonly, I hear lists containing cooking, listening to music, talking to their family, running, and praying. These activities can be self-regulating in times of stress and are great opportunities to practice mindfulness and take account of what brings them joy and gratitude. Formal evaluation and constructive criticism are a common source of stress for students in the field. I have found authentic task practice to be a useful strategy. In class, I explain to students that the early evaluations are formal but formative and that the final summative one is more significant because it depicts growth throughout the semester. One way to encourage growth is to become receptive to feedback. To nurture that capacity, we practice. I assign students an exercise to research, plan, teach, and assess a mini-lesson for our class, similar to what they will be asked to do in the field. Their peers, who serve as their students in the lesson, provide them feedback on the lesson using the actual content evaluation forms used by the department to assess students teaching in the field. The feedback is provided immediately in written and verbal form, and it can sometimes be tough to hear. Throughout the exercise, I remind students that the goal of the exercise is to find opportunities for growth and that the feedback can only be viewed as positive if they are open to that stance. I find that the more opportunities students have to freely talk and hear about the work, the more comfortable and productive the work becomes.

After every significant exercise or experience, students write a reflection. Reflection in EL is seen as "the internal transformation of an experience" (Kolb, 2015, p. 58); however, even in this part of the Experiential Learning Cycle, I find that students often benefit from support strategies. I almost always provide a process, using guiding questions, for students to follow as they reflect. I begin by asking them to write about how they feel after completing an activity; I find that this is a crucial step to transition their thinking from an emotional stance to a logical one. Next, I ask students to take another perspective to think how others may have experienced the activity; often, they have data or feedback to consider. I then ask students to consider changes they would make if doing the activity again. Finally, I ask them to detail the next step; do they need to learn more about a topic, follow-up with anyone, implement a strategy, or ask questions. At the end of a course, one student wrote:

> After taking a moment to reflect on all of the feedback I have received this semester, I can honestly say that this is the most beneficial education course I have taken so far... it helped me to grow as an educator. Seeing where I struggled in building the lesson was a great source of information to help me begin to improve. (Student reflection, November 2020)

Beyond focusing on intrinsic aspects and doing intrapersonal work, another helpful support strategy that comes from the Learning Paradigm is that of a community of practice, a type of Learning Community.

Lenning et al. (2013) describe a Learning Community as "an intentionally developed community that exists to promote and maximize the individual and shared learning of its members. There is ongoing interaction, interplay, and collaboration among the community's members as they strive for specified common learning goals" (2013, p. 7). Our AYA team functions as a Learning Community, especially during students' senior year. There is a common calendar, and we get together in several different capacities. We meet for team seminars and may even share a meal. Other times, we get together outside of a class structure to have an all-team workday where we work in community on common but individual tasks. In addition, students typically have a shared phone text thread and

frequently meet each other outside of class. It is a team, and we all participate, help each other, and hold each other accountable.

SUPPORTING STUDENTS EXPERIENCING ACADEMIC
AND PROFESSIONAL DEMANDS

There are times when students are challenged by a daunting academic
task. For my students, it is an in-depth, long-term, online portfolio of
their teaching activities prior to graduation. As an AYA team, we do our
best to prepare students for known challenges, so for this task, professors
in each content area commit to assign a mini-portfolio the semester prior.
In this authentic practice strategy, students gain necessary knowledge and
learn potential pitfalls prior to the main task. We have found the coordination and commitment that have been worthwhile as students have not
been as overwhelmed or intimidated by the requirements.

Despite my best efforts, there are times when I cannot foresee challenges or do not have the time to prepare students for every scenario. For
example, as a liaison, one of my students was unexpectedly assigned to
teach a Psychology class, and she quickly became aware of gaps in her
content knowledge. When students are confronted with an academic or
professional challenge, I strongly encourage them to take the initiative to
talk with their content professors and CEs prior to involving me. Part of
learning and being successful in EL is taking an active role to articulate
and solve their own problems; however, when they need more support, I
primarily use guided questioning. I ask them to explain the predicament,
identify the core problem, make connections to what they know and what
has worked in other situations, list what resources might be needed, and
ultimately make a plan of action, which is what my student had to do to
catch-up on the Psychology content as she was teaching. I have found that
this strategy can encourage students to use independent thinking, and it
also promotes higher orders of thinking.

Beyond the use of support strategies, the AYA course sequence is scaffolded to support students. In their junior year, the lab component is
graded pass or fail. In their senior year, they receive a letter grade for student teaching. Evaluation is also scaffolded. The department encourages
pre-observation and post-observation conferences, which I view as paramount to the evaluation process. At the pre-observation conference, I
choose questions that provide students an opportunity to explain their

process and class context. I ask them what they feel most confident about, what concerns they have, and what they would like me to know or to focus upon so that I can best support them. It is imperative for me to know the context in which they are working, such as if they have a struggling student, or their class will have an assembly interruption, or the learning management system has intermittent Wi-Fi. They may even tell me that they have not been feeling well or have not taken the time necessary to plan. I am often surprised at their honesty, but I think that given the space, they want to have the conversation.

For the post-observation conference, I provide positive feedback and highlight opportunities for growth. I remind them that my role is to help them do their best, learn, and grow. I then ask them for their thoughts on the lesson. Typically, they mention many of the things that I had written down to discuss; they know where they struggled and where they excelled. Then there is a great opportunity to inquire how they can use that knowledge to guide future instruction. For the areas that they need to improve upon, we craft a plan of action. There is a space at the bottom of their lesson plan format for them to write a reflection once they get home that day and have time to collect their thoughts. Time for honest and thorough reflection is an integral part of the development process.

The Importance of Monitoring and Encouraging Reciprocal Relationships

Teaching students in the classroom and visiting them in the field provides many opportunities to see, talk, teach, learn, and check on them, but there is much time when they are working without me physically present. Instead, they have a CE who serves in those capacities. Student teachers work within a secondary school community, interacting with faculty, administrators, staff, and parents. They are also assigned a university liaison to help bridge the gap between the secondary school and the university.

Even with the help of their professors, their CE, and their liaison, students can still struggle with the complex nature of maintaining so many relationships. All of the stakeholders have some impact on student teaching tasks, such as learning content, planning for creatively teaching that content, meeting individual student needs, choosing and using technology tools, creating assessments, analyzing data, managing a classroom, and completing student teaching licensing requirements. While it is ultimately a gift to have so much field input, it can also lead to feeling overwhelmed. Students also experience administrative-type challenges, such as keeping track of requirements and navigating conflicting work styles, advice, or practices. One student commented during student teaching, "My CE's classroom was mainly lecture-based, so instituting different activities within the class was harder because I didn't want to mess-up or alter the flow and structure of the class."

Support Strategies to Help Students Build Reciprocal Relationships

I utilize various support strategies to encourage relationship-building. In the classroom, for example, I have students create a "Learning Community Agreement" in which they collectively describe their values and expected norms of the class. It typically includes items such as the level of lighting and music, what snacks are allowed, the calendar, accountability, times for talking, and class breaks. This creates a comfortable place for them to connect and learn. One student wrote a letter to the next year's students, offering advice on the importance of relationships:

> You are probably trying to figure out how you will be able to balance your schoolwork, your social life, and your need to sleep/eat…Class, you all need to stick together. You're all the new "Language Squad." You will rely on one another for ideas, consolation, and straight up mutual understanding…I believe in you! P.S. If you need a motivation playlist, let me know. (Student reflection, April 2019)

As students transition from a student role to a professional one, building reciprocal relationships with other professionals and community members is a valuable endeavor. These relationships serve as a support system and also help students to perceive themselves as legitimate and contributing members to the profession. There are a couple support strategies that I have found to be particularly useful in this endeavor.

First, prior to student teaching, I arrange for students to participate in clinical rounds at a local high school. In this experience, students enter a reciprocal relationship with two CEs. The CEs provide topics of inquiry, based upon data that they would like collected, such as "How are literary strategies being implemented; are they effective?" or "How are teachers holding all students accountable for their learning?" My students then meet with the CEs, who describe their class, their instructional decisions, and even disclose their concerns for the lesson. Students then act as silent, yet active, observers in each classroom as they record relevant data. The experience culminates with a debrief to share their findings. The relationship is reciprocal in that students have an opportunity to engage in professional conversations and to hear how a teacher reflects. In turn, students offer CEs valuable information that they are often not able to collect themselves. Several teachers over the years have continued relationships with my students beyond the semester, offering them resources and advice, inviting them into the teaching community.

Second, when students are further along in their program, I encourage them to get to know people at their field placement. Simple behaviors such as arriving early, asking questions, communicating challenges, and expressing gratitude can promote community building. One day I arrived at a school and was greeted by an administrator who told me what a pleasure it was to have UD student teachers at their school. In contrast, one day I encountered a CE who was angry due to the student teacher's miscommunication about an absence. Reciprocal relationships are not only significant for student teachers but also for the future of the program.

SUPPORT STRATEGIES TO HELP STUDENTS CONNECT WITH FIELD EXPERTS

In addition to building relationships in the field, students benefit from connections to other experts who can provide academic and professional support, encouraging a community of practice. To support those relationships, I connect students with campus support services and professional organizations as early as possible. Having a relationship with the Office of Career Services, for example, makes it more likely that students will fully utilize the services and ask for assistance when they need it. Likewise, professional organizations connect new teachers to a larger community and to a multitude of resources, advice, workshops, and conferences that make information more timely and accessible. To encourage students to make these connections, I assign projects and student-led conferences based on what they learned from professional organizations and on what issues about which they have become passionate. These connections and passions can also offer students additional motivation to persevere.

In the field, CEs and liaisons serve as experts. These connections must stay strong to help students feel fully supported and avoid feeling disconnected. However, there are times when students receive contradictory messages about expectations. For example, students are required to prepare detailed lesson plans, but a CE may recommend a shorter version of planning. This is an opportunity to discuss with the student the evolution of becoming a veteran teacher and the choices that come with increased skills. I have found that increasing my presence in the field, even if informally, is a useful strategy in discovering small concerns before they become large ones. I make it a habit to do a quick walk by my students' classrooms anytime that I am in the building. It reminds students that I am accessible and is an opportunity for them to inform me of any issues. Many times, I just stop in for a quick hello and later send an email to let them know how confident they looked while teaching or how great the projects were hanging up in the room. It is important for them to know that my role is to encourage and support them, not just to evaluate them.

The triad relationship between myself, the student teacher, and the CE is also of importance. We meet at midterm and finals to evaluate student teachers' pedagogy and disposition. At the meeting, we all submit rubric scores and then use data to come to a consensus on the scoring of each item. Students often underrate themselves or have anxiety about what their scores might be, but the conversations with experts in the field become a support strategy in which students hear positive feedback about what they are doing well and should continue doing. They also receive focused feedback on the areas that are opportunities for growth, and the meeting concludes with goal setting.

APPLYING LEARNING TO NEW CHALLENGES

Institutions of higher education can encourage student growth by offering EL opportunities. The experiences can be transformative when consisting of authentic experiences that place students in an active role. After setting up the conditions necessary and sending students out into the field, students will require support along the way that is appropriate for the specific challenges they will face. I have found it helpful to identify common challenges and then to use the learning paradigm to select which support strategies will be most useful to students. Based on my experience of teaching and supporting students progressing from interns to student teachers, and through my study of constructive developmental growth, I have found many practices to be useful and had much experience to draw upon. However, I was caught off guard when COVID-19 changed all of our work. One of UD's mission and identity themes, Theme 3: Educating for Practical Wisdom, "allows one to read the signs of the times and to be skillful in adaptation and change...evaluate the trends of our society... seek justice, peace, reconciliation and the common good...(and) develop a sense of purpose and meaning in their lives and to continually refine that purpose into a deeper sense of vocation" (p. 19). I thought of this thread often, as adaptation became paramount beginning in the spring of 2020.

Students have had to teach differently, in a way that they have never been taught. They have had new struggles as one student lamented:

> Although this is not possible in our current world, I wish the students could have been closer together (when working in groups) so they would have an actual discussion about the questions and what the answers might be. To supplement this for now, we could set up a way for students to communicate their discussion with their partners via technology, like Google Chat. (Student reflection, November 2020)

The remote teaching that they have had to learn in the field will certainly serve them well going forward, as some of the adaptations may be here to stay.

In addition to professional struggles, new and more intense personal challenges became apparent this past year, unique for each student. I have students who lost family members, who themselves became ill with the virus, who faced mental health crises, and whose family responsibilities greatly increased. Nearly all students had a change in their living arrangements. Having to give up independence and moving back home as a young adult is not what students or their families had planned. Not only did students need additional support as they dealt with unforeseen personal challenges, but my role became a remote one. I had my own family challenges, concern for my students' well-being, and still the accountability for preparing teachers. Students still had to continue with their program, graduate, get their Ohio teaching license, and enter their first teaching job in the fall.

For my juniors, I had to increase my own capacity to create remote field experiences for them. I spent much time deconstructing the value gained from the field and then attempting to reconstruct it remotely. Students needed personalized learning during the pandemic, so I began by having them create a goal based on what they needed to be prepared for the subsequent semester. Then I provided choices for activities that they could select to meet their goal and to fulfill the lab component. Personally, I have not had quite enough reflection time to offer much wisdom on how to teach during a pandemic, and in fact, I am still learning and doing so as I type. My Zoom class meeting with my current student interns ended today with my audio cutting out, leading to a premature end of the Zoom meeting and a move to typing asynchronously in a chat forum with subsequent emails. But what I have been heartened to see is a community that comes together with understanding. A student contacted me after the unproductive class to let me know to not worry because it could have happened to anyone, and that she was certain that I have given grace to others in similar situations. I can only believe that reaction comes from a foundation created far before a crisis. We are a community of learners, and despite change, we continue to learn and grow together.

REFERENCES

Association for Experiential Education. (2020). *What is experiential education?* Retrieved from https://www.aee.org/what-is-ee

Barr, R. B., & Tagg, J. (1995). From teaching to learning: A new paradigm for undergraduate education. *Change, 27*(6), 12–26.

Baxter Magolda, M. B. (2007). Self-authorship: The foundation for twenty-first-century education. *New Directions for Teaching & Learning, 109,* 69–83.

Common Themes in the Mission and Identity of the University of Dayton. Mission and Identity Task Force, 2010–2012. Common Themes in the Mission and Identity of the University of Dayton.pdf.

Kegan, R. (1982). *The evolving self: Problem and process in human development.* Harvard University.

Kegan, R. (1994). *In over our heads: The mental demands of modern life.* Harvard University.

Kolb, D. A. (1984). *Experiential learning: Experience as the source of learning and development.* Prentice Hall.

Kolb, D. A. (2015). *Experiential learning: Experience as the source of learning and development* (2nd ed.). Pearson Education Ltd..

Lenning, O. T., Hill, D. M., Saunders, K. P., Solan, A., & Stokes, A. (2013). *Powerful learning communities: A guide to developing student, faculty, and professional learning communities to improve student success and organizational effectiveness.* Stylus Publishing, LLC.

Linehan, M. M. (2015). *DPT skills training: Handouts and worksheets* (2nd ed.). Guildford Press.

Mahler, E. B. (2011). Midlife work role transitions: Generativity and learning in 21st-century careers. In C. Hoare (Ed.), *The Oxford handbook of reciprocal adult development and learning* (2nd ed., pp. 186–214). Oxford University Press.

Palmer, P. J. (2007). *The courage to teach: Exploring the inner landscape of a teacher's life.* Jossey-Bass.

Tagg, J. (2003). *The learning paradigm college.* Anker.

CHAPTER 14

Afterword: Reflecting on Post-COVID Experiential Education and Learning

Kevin Dvorak and Mario D'Agostino

This collection of essays provides a broad range of experiential learning (EL) activities students experience while in college. From internships to service learning, to working with non-profits or for-profits, students should have the opportunity to learn outside of the classroom, to get hands-on experience, and to spend time reflecting on those experiences. As the field of EL has grown significantly over the last 40 years, it has developed many best practices, as have been noted throughout *Diverse Pedagogical Approaches to EL (Volume 2)*. However, these best practices were disrupted by the COVID-19 pandemic, leaving most, if not all, experiential educators unsure how to proceed, at least initially. As noted by

K. Dvorak (✉)
Writing and Communication Center; Communication, Media, and the Arts, Nova Southeastern University, Ft. Lauderdale, FL, USA
e-mail: kdvorak@nova.edu

M. D'Agostino
Communication, Media, and the Arts, Nova Southeastern University, Ft. Lauderdale, FL, USA
e-mail: mdagost0@nova.edu

K. Lovett (ed.), *Diverse Pedagogical Approaches to Experiential Learning, Volume II*,
https://doi.org/10.1007/978-3-030-83688-7_14

197

several authors in this collection, such as Dickey; Cardilino, Kennedy, and Niebler; and Rogan-Floom, COVID-19 caught experiential educators "off guard" as it "suspended" work, and it left many "wondering" how to continue their efforts. Now, a year into the pandemic, with an eye on returning to some sense of normalcy, we offer ideas for the future of EL, based largely on adjustments colleagues have made to their programs and how the global workforce has rapidly evolved in response to the coronavirus.

In only one year, the world of work has changed more dramatically than, perhaps, any other 365-day period in modern history. This past year, faculty, administrators, and students have found themselves stuck in a liminal space; a space where forceful transition required us to reflect on what once was and to consider what will now follow. As the designers of experiential education, faculty, and/or administrators need to recognize how the global workforce has evolved, primarily in regard to the types of careers our students strive for, and adjust opportunities so that they continue to prepare students for these changes.

One of the most prominent ways the workforce has changed has been the acceleration of telework, or working remotely, especially from home. As we move past COVID-19, it is likely that corporations and employers will continue developing ways for employees to spend less time (or no time) at the office in an effort to cut down on overhead and improve productivity through the increased flexibility working remotely provides employees. To that end, we can expect our students to have three options for working when they enter their careers: fully onsite, hybrid, and fully remote. Experiential educators have long provided the skills students need for onsite work—just take a look at the chapters in this collection!—but it is now time to consider how traditional EL activities might proceed by providing students with hybrid and remote opportunities.

HYBRID AND FULLY REMOTE WORK: NEW REQUIRED SKILLS

Hybrid work allows employees to spend part of their time working onsite and the other part working remotely. Onsite, colleagues have opportunities to get to know one another—to create community—while in person, hopefully developing strong professional bonds and trust that support them while working away from each other. In contrast, fully remote work allows an employee to work completely away from a centralized office—if there even is one. Whereas onsite and hybrid works allow employees to have the chance to develop community in person with colleagues, fully remote work challenges employees to develop these bonds using various technologies, particularly web-based conferencing platforms and team-based messaging apps. Thus, both hybrid and fully remote works require employees to develop new skill sets, and it may behoove experiential educators to focus on some of these to best prepare students for their careers. Below, we list some of these critical skills (some of which are adapted from the National Association for Colleges and Employers) and how remote EL activities can provide students with opportunities to develop them. While each of these skills is also fundamental to onsite employment, each takes on a different meaning when working remotely.

- **Communication**: From web-conferencing platforms to text messaging apps to phone calls, communication is critical to the success of remote workers. There is a greater need for clarity and for learning the nuances of virtual communication. Over the past year, both our written and spoken practices have undergone changes, and we as practitioners need to be cognizant of this shift to ensure that instructions and expectations are properly communicated.
- **Technology/Digital Literacy**: Remote workers depend entirely on technology, usually multiple technologies, to complete their work. This generates a greater dependence on understanding how to use more types of hardware and software, thinking critically about how technologies work, and how to troubleshoot problems quickly when they arise.
- **Time Management/Initiative**: While flexibility may sound good, it does not always translate into getting a job done on time. Remote work means not working in physical proximity to colleagues who will hold each other accountable. There is an aspect of self-directedness to this type of work, and remote workers need to stay motivated and organized to meet deadlines.
- **Collaboration**: Students should learn how to facilitate virtual meetings and be part of working teams that communicate primarily through virtual and written means. Remote work may force employees to work closely with people they only communicate with asynchronously via email; that is certainly not the case for collaborating in traditional work settings.
- **Intercultural Fluency**: Remote work increases the possibility of working with more diverse colleagues from around the country and

world. Understanding how to communicate professionally and how to build collegiality and trust solely through digital means can be more complicated than working onsite. There are fewer informal moments to develop an understanding of and appreciation for colleagues.

- **Community**: Employees need to build trust in one another to be highly effective and to enjoy job satisfaction. Building community happens beyond just completing tasks with one another; it requires socializing before or during a break in a remote meeting. It happens by offering praise to another colleague via email or messaging app.

POST-COVID EXPERIENTIAL OPPORTUNITIES: QUESTIONS FOR FACULTY AND ADMINISTRATORS

Of course, decisions about EL need to include partners from the places where students gain their experience, and these conversations should also include the students themselves. We can also consider the Eight Principles of Good Practice for All Experiential Learning Activities, promoted by the National Society for Experiential Education (n.d.), and The Principles of Practice recognized by the Association for Experiential Education (n.d.), when developing questions about how to incorporate remote work into EL.

- How much of the experiential opportunity can be remote? Depending on the length of the activity, is it possible to build in a progression, beginning fully onsite and then transitioning to hybrid or fully remote?
- What kind of preparations for the experience can take place remotely, through learning management systems or other web-based learning tools, in order to prepare the student?
- What skills do we want students to focus on while working remotely? How can we make remote working meaningful?
- How can we build in effective strategies for remote monitoring and remote assessment? If students work remotely, should they be communicating with advisors remotely?
- How do we pay careful attention to issues of potential inequity? How do we ensure that if students have chances to work remotely, they also have the appropriate materials, technologies, access points, and workspaces to be effective?

- How do we educate and train students to work remotely? Remote work tends to favor those with more knowledge and experience, so how do we provide initial skills that will help students to be successful?

CONCLUSION

This afterword hopes to address a looming, lumbering question: where do experiential educators go from here? We understand that one of the main goals of EL is to prepare students to be successful in the workforce and that we, as practitioners and administrators, must meet the demands of this changing landscape to ensure that students are placed in the very best position to succeed. In this afterword, we have outlined items for instructors to consider when moving a rich, onsite EL activity to a remote or hybrid format. We have also outlined questions for practitioners to consider when deciding if it is even possible to pivot a specific course/program from an in-person to online format (beginning, here, with course learning outcomes/objectives and whether these need to be amended/reconciled as we shift from one modality to another).

Of course, we understand that not all courses/programs will translate to the modalities outlined above. As important voices featured in this collection have noted (e.g., Sayre; Willenbrink-Conte; Fine and McLoughlin; LaDuca and Ausdenmoore, to name a few), internships, community-engaged learning, and hands-on experiments/simulations can pose unique challenges that make it difficult to mimic activities remotely. For example, our NSU Composition, Rhetoric, and Digital Media (CRDM) Master's Program has hosted a front-facing, in-person gallery exhibit that curates the work our graduate students completed throughout the academic year. Understanding that CDC guidelines would not allow for this type of exhibition last summer, we used different technologies at our disposal (such as Adobe Illustrator and In-Design, as well as web-hosting platforms like ThingLink) to create a virtually walkable gallery space that still enabled us to achieve the initial goal of the in-person exhibition. "*In MEDIAs Res*" (Mason & D'Agostino 2020) was the result of decisions made with haste in the face of an enormous, unprecedented situation. What resulted was a hyper-sensory and multisensory online colloquium that featured the students' dynamic digital and material content while celebrating their ingenuity. Students who would otherwise be working in a gallery were asked to work remotely, design, and collaborate with faculty without being in person. Along with asking students to consider the curatorial techniques of design, placement, and embodied narratives, the great thing about a digital exhibit is that it lives on. Readers of this collection could visit "In MEDIAs Res" whereas only those who were in the Fort Lauderdale area could attend an in-person exhibition.

We share this anecdote because it augments how our typical experiences have had to evolve over the past year. There are other stories and testimonies like this that exemplify how to create immersive learning environments in remote or hybrid settings. We hope that the perspectives offered here energize this collection's readers and give them tools and ideas for carrying forward. We have all performed the important work that has helped answer the question "where do we go from here?" May this collegiality and supportiveness carry us past the unique challenges that await the post-COVID world.

References

Association for Experiential Education. (n.d.). *Experiential education: The principles of practice*. https://www.aee.org/what-is-ee

Mason, E., & D'Agostino, M. (2020). *In MEDIAS Res: A C.R.D.M. Colloquium*. Retrieved March 21, 2021, from https://www.thinglink.com/video/1337073781323071489?editor-closed

National Association of Colleges and Employers. (n.d.). *Career competencies defined*. https://www.naceweb.org/career-readiness/competencies/career-readiness-defined/

National Society for Experiential Education. (n.d.). *Eight principles of good practice for all experiential learning activities*. https://www.nsee.org/8-principles